The *Mentor* Within

Let your *SELF* be seen

ISBN: 0-9767485-0-9

The Mentor Within

Let your *SELF* be seen

Mary Gerard

PROJECT
HEALING
PRESS

CONTENTS

*   *   *

In the following pages, Mary Gerard's questions and comments are in normal typeface and **The Mentor Within answers in bold typeface.**

*   *   *

PREFACE

The Three Invitations

My spiritual options appeared to be diminishing quickly and my hope for a sense of purpose in life as well. How, after a lifetime of devotion to my spiritual journey, had I arrived at such a place of futility and despair. Nothing was working. My relationships felt meaningless, stagnant, and I no longer recognized myself within them. My job which I had returned to graduate school for at 35 years of age after a shattered marriage and all the dreams attached to it dismantled as well, was dulling my mind at the speed of light. Life seemed to hold little hope and unfulfilling answers to my questions.

One evening I lied in bed reading *Open Mind Open Heart*, by Thomas Keating, a monk, abbot, and founder of Centering Prayer which I have practiced. He mentioned the spiritual exercises of a mystic, St. Ignatius of Loyola. "I would be willing to do those," a still Voice inside me spoke, "whatever they are, sounds interesting." The next day I arrived for my appointment with my therapist, Paul, who really functioned more as my spiritual director. What a godsend he had been in the midst of this confusion. As I sat my heaviness down and looked at him with eyes of doubt, he leaned over, lifted a brochure from the table beside me, and handed it to me. "I think you might find this interesting, Mary," he said assuredly with a glimmer in his eye. Glancing down to peruse the brochure, I see the writing, "*BRIDGES: The Spiritual Exercises of St. Ignatius of Loyola.*" I burst into laughter sharing with Paul what I had just read the night before. The deadline to sign-up was a couple of days away. There are no accidents!

I knew immediately that I was being called to a deeper level of relationship with my Self. Without a thought I agreed within to commit to the nine month program. I am sure I had been called any number of ways prior to this, but was not willing to listen and/or follow. The form of one's spiritual calling takes on many shapes and reveals itself to us constantly, awaiting our response. It wasn't that the Spiritual Exercises were "the way," rather I was willing to say yes in that moment to the Voice beckoning me, "Come, spend some time with Me, Mary." This was the first invitation. I accepted.

Nine months later. Yes, a deepened relationship with the Divine had rooted its Self within me and I came to know myself anew. Now what? The Newness within had planted its seed, but I was expecting to be fully blossomed after nine months. Divine timing supercedes once again. Though admittedly, I had no desire to emerge from my cocoon. I had come to know the beauty of resting in God's presence. Beliefs had been shattered as I came to know God beyond beliefs and formal teachings. Still, so many questions I was longing to ask. Maybe further studies, I imagined, would change my external world and I would finally find my place.

A breezy summer evening in May at a spontaneous family dinner at Bar Italia in St. Louis' Central West End, my significant other John, becoming impatient with my perpetual search for Light, Love, and my Self, put his two cents in. "Mary," he smiled, "You hear the Voice of truth absolutely clearly Guiding you through life, yet you continue to ignore it; not only do you ignore it, you actually hear the answers to your questions with great clarity and then turn and do the exact opposite! You do not need more studies in the world. You need to write a book. This book will be your final certificate and your final diploma!" That is it I thought. I always knew within me that someday I would write a book, but had not the faintest idea as to the subject matter.

As I went within in prayer to contemplate this suggestion, I knew the familiar Voice within saying, "Mary, come and ask Me your questions. I have the answers you have been looking for." Here was the second invitation. Once again, without hesitation, I accepted. Before I could even fully formulate the question in my mind as to the title of the book, I heard the Voice answer, "*The Mentor Within.*" Wow, that is it! My whole life I had been searching for a mentor. Though some individuals had their mentoring moments and others were candidates, no one ever fully lived up to my expectations of a mentor. Well, of course not. Because I was never really looking for a mentor, I was looking for my Self. I was searching the world for my Self, the divine grace of God resting in stillness within.

After nine months of resting in solitude, silence, and Holy Spirit's wisdom, asking my questions and listening for the answers, I came into my Self. The Self I was being called to claim and be a witness to. The Self I am. Now here I rest. A third knock at the door patiently waits for me, invitation in hand. I open the door. I open the invitation, I hear the Voice, "Mary, let your Self be seen and I will be seen along with you." I answer the call. As I open to the Christ within, I am opening to my Self.

Mary Gerard

INTRODUCTION

The Mentor Within is the Voice of Self, our true nature that is still aware of Its connection to God. It is readily available if we are willing to listen. Moving in and out of awareness of this Voice my entire life, I begin to notice that the Voice seems to be seeking me. Forever I had chosen not to follow the wisdom of the Mentor Within for it rarely seemed to concur with the "wisdom" of the world. However, the "wisdom" of the world began sounding like the robotic voices that call my home leaving programmed messages on the answering machine. There was nothing real about it. I had fallen for the promises of a programmed illusion. Angry, frustrated, disappointed and fed up with everything the material and even so-called "spiritual" world had to offer, I began giving up. No person, place, situation or thing brought me the real peace and happiness for which I longed and knew within myself had to exist.

The Mentor Within is the daily, written account of the past nine months of my inner listening as I engaged in a discussion with this Voice, asking questions and listening for the answers. These questions pertain to common day-to-day situations including dealing with issues at my place of work, how to use my time and prioritize my activities, how to maneuver through the world and make the best use of my interactions, and looking at the reasoning and intention behind my choices. The Mentor Within also speaks to my inquiries about the purpose of my life, the reason for and meaning of my relationships, my adhering to family and societal expectations, and what is God's Will for me. Other questions include who is Jesus, the Christ, and the Holy Spirit, and why all the suffering and persecution in the world like the Holocaust. The Mentor teaches me how to recognize and be freed from the false self.

As I enter into this conversation, the Mentor Within answers my questions in ways that lead me to further questioning. Also, I realize that though my questions are of a personal nature, the Mentor Within gives answers which have a universal application. This is one way I knew I was hearing the Voice of truth; the Mentor Within does not seek to solve my individual problems with individual solutions that only apply to my situation. The Mentor Within is not interested in self-help, rather revealing the Self. For it is in revealing the Self that I realize that the root of all of my problems, my restless mind, and unhappiness, is my false self who is unable to see, hear, or know the truth. The false self will never find God because the false self wants to be God.

My whole world is turned upside down as the Mentor Within shows me how my perceptions of the world, others and myself are constantly shifting; dependent on my thoughts, mood, emotional state, the weather, learned beliefs and value systems, societal expectations, cultural norms, religious upbringing ... Nothing is as it seems to appear as I realize the unceasing changeability and instability of my perceptions. I enter an identity crisis as I realize the power of my false self and its insidious nature as it seeks to keep me searching for happiness and peace in the world only to be disappointed again and again. The creed of the false self, the ego, is stated clearly in *A Course in Miracles*, "seek and do not find." The Mentor Within, as my true Self, guides me out of the maze of darkened dead ends, taking me on an inner journey where I come to realize that real peace and happiness can only be found within; the Kingdom of Heaven lies within.

To hear the guidance of the Mentor Within during the course of this writing, I began each period of listening with becoming quiet within, calling upon the Holy Spirit and asking to be drawn into the presence of God, to hear not the voices of the world or even my own voice, but the Voice of truth. I do not enter a trance-like state in order to hear this Voice, rather I am in a heightened level of awareness by choice and willingness to surrender my mind to God.

As my willingness and commitment to listening have grown, I am now able to hear the Mentor Within without relying on pen and paper. I choose whether or not to let the wisdom speak through me or to "do it my way." Inevitably, 100 percent of the time, "my way" is no match for the ways and words of the Mentor Within, as the Voice of my true Self.

While asking the questions, answers came easily and quickly. If I begin to struggle hearing the answers, I put the pen down. I am clearly able to distinguish between my voice and the Voice of the Mentor Within. The Mentor Within will give me the answer **one word at a time**. I may think I know the entire sentence, but a quite different idea ends up on paper as I let the Mentor guide my thoughts. Also, the false self tends to jump in and answer the question immediately with a loud, overbearing tone. The Mentor Within is recognized as the still, small Voice that rises up from a *knowing* that is not of the intellect, emotions, cultural conditioning, habit, learned beliefs, or a value system.

Hearing the answers of the Mentor Within requires a "listening" unlike how we would define listening in the world. This is a listening without judgment or preconceived notions. It is not necessary to turn down the environmental noise that I usually desire for listening. I am able to clearly hear the Mentor's Voice even amidst loud music, clanging dishes, and other's talking. Furthermore, my inner response to the answers of the false self is fleeting excitement or fear, whereas my experience of the Mentor's Voice is one of inner peace and recognition of truth.

Much of this conversation is inspired by my search for my spiritual calling as I witness my life and the lives of those around me which all appear to be lacking in some fundamental way. What are the obstacles to my responding to God's Will? Why do I always have one foot out the door? The Mentor Within does not mince words as It directly responds that the first order of business if I am to respond to my spiritual calling, is that I must commit to my own healing.

The Mentor speaks, **"You are your first client."**

May this book serve as a demonstration, reminder, and inspiration to be willing to listen to the Voice of our true Self within.

Grace of God

"Grace becomes inevitable instantly
in those who have prepared a table
where it can be gently laid and willingly received."

A Course in Miracles

I cannot go on another day
living as if I do not
hear the truth.

Chapter
One: May

It is not outside of ourselves.
Whatever we are looking for,
is not outside of ourselves.

I ask God, "What is it you want me to say (in this book)"? God responds, *"I want you to tell the truth."*

I cannot go on another day living as if I do not hear the truth. It is taking my breath away. The world has its own take on truth and it is a "truth" that perpetuates falseness. Much of my life has been expending energy to stay in line with that which is not true. Whenever I contemplated stepping out of the one dimensional line of this world, and did so, the pain of having to return was excruciating. The joy of the moment of escape was fleeting, for I quickly felt pulled back into the supposed security of the line. Full of doubt, I questioned, "How secure could this level of joy possibly be? Can I count on it still being there tomorrow morning when I awake?"

I know for a fact that I can count on the misery of the world to provide me with enough material for a lifetime. I can build my life around it, analyze it, develop plans on how to resolve it, talk to friends, family, and therapists around the clock. It is a misery so pervasive that we will do anything not to feel it; we will numb out, have more children, buy more cars, get into more debt, go back to school, go shopping, make more commitments to our work and church, drink, eat, exercise, watch television, become a member on yet another board, have more sex, make more money, attempt to make even more money, move across the country, redecorate, talk, talk some more ... The list is endless. We will fake every moment of our lives to not have to feel this misery. This was the thinking of my darker moments. There was one way out.

*   *   *

Do You Hear?

It is on this day that I am given the title of the book. The Mentor begins to speak.

It is not outside of ourselves — whatever we are looking for is not outside of ourselves. We are making ourselves sick

looking for answers out there in a world where there are no answers. Oh yes, we may be temporarily satisfied, have an "aha" moment, but are you not fleeting frantically to the next endeavor, experience, goal, guru, friend, family member, therapist, doctor, financial advisor, church, book, job ...? Are you not feeling anxious, lost, depressed, numb, out of control, in control, controlling between gurus?

How many gurus does it take to screw in a light bulb? There will never be enough, because the Light is within. The peace of God is within. The moment of truth is within. You will feel whole when you accept that no one outside of you can make you whole — you are in fact complete because God completed you before you were born. Nothing or no one in this world can complete you who are already finished. Additions make for distractions.

How many rooms does a house need before it is a home? How many blades of grass does a field need before it can be called a field? I am telling you; one room makes a home, one blade of grass on a spot of land makes a field. You are that room, you are that blade of grass; you are home, you are a field. Nothing else matters.

Life will unfold as we listen. Do you hear the sound of your own unfolding? What a gift.

I cannot make anything happen. I can only be a gift to that which is already happening. It is the greatest freedom I have.

*   *   *

There Will Never Be Another You

Not long ago I found myself a prisoner of my own mind and all of its extensions. A tangled web of inroads and outposts. Passing by myself at the speed of light. Coveting my extensions, darkening the already shady corners, filling in the blanks with multiple choice questions ... should I end that statement with an exclamation point, maybe a question mark, or how about a semicolon? Apparently there is a right answer, but what is it? I could put each of these answers on trial, give a good defense, and justify every one. Stay neutral, yeah, that's it, I will be neutral. I will stay glued to my neutrality, like the color beige. Beige never bothered anybody and it blends in nicely. Tuesday morning, I wake up with my hands on my head. God, I can't be beige. Do you see the vicious cycle? Never quite right, never quite good enough. I am exhausted.

I have been sensing a knowing inside of myself since I was a little girl. I first experienced it as an upsurge of movement or energy beginning in my belly and shooting out the top of my head. One time when I was about nine years old I asked a few people if they ever felt such a thing. I got a "no" and a real clarity that they had no idea what I was talking about. I decided to not ask anybody this question any more and just go on feeling the exhilaration of these energy surges sweeping me with joy.

As I grew older, I had occasional energy surges and frequently noticed an awareness inside of me that seemed to have a sense of knowing on another level, not at a cognitive level or something I learned in school. However, it was helpful to me in the world of decision making and taking action, when I trusted it. Herein is the key phrase, "when I trusted it." This still, small voice was often drowned out by the louder voice of authority of the world.

Into my college years, I began to feel bombarded by what was expected of me in terms of joining up with the world so I could be "successful." All of a sudden, or so it seemed, the whole concept of the "real world" and how everyone around me were living their lives seemed bizarre. I was not in sync. My friends sat around the cafeteria table perusing college catalogs and deciding on their majors. Are you kidding, I thought? I am only nineteen years old. I am supposed to choose one thing and do it for the rest of my life or at least until I married and had children? This was insanity; surely there had been a mistake and I had gotten off on the wrong planet. At that moment sitting around the cafeteria table with my friends, I remember hearing an inner Voice whispering to me, "There will never be another you."

Even as I write this book about the answers being within and a limitless amount of knowledge being within, even now that I have completed many studies including psychology, dance, occupational therapy, movement, bodywork, meditation, spirituality, and more, I am still searching for an outer mentor to learn even more. The pull to find a mentor outside of me is still so strong and at the same time disturbing because I feel like one of those rats going through a behavioral psychology experiment employing intermittent reinforcement. They tolerate an aversive stimulus like electrical shock because they are given food as positive reinforcement at frequent enough intervals to sustain them. Eventually they develop "learned helplessness," which is an apathetic state; they give up. This occurs often in human beings as well. Under aversive, stressful conditions we become conditioned to ignore our instincts about what is best for us and tap into our inner resources because we are given just enough nourishment to sustain us, just enough positive reinforcement to keep us hanging in. We become locked up in a vicious cycle of tolerating unhappiness and looking outside of ourselves for nourishment.

*   *   *

Who is the Mentor Within?

I remember my mother saying to me years ago, "Mary, why are you always going outside of your self looking for the answer? You know the answer."

The Mentor Within is that inner, still Voice that seeks me, that draws me out of my shell. It makes itself known at all hours of the day and night. It has no enemies, for love is all it has to give. If I forget what the Mentor Within has told me, it will remind me as many times as I need reminding. It has a way of showing itself to me out of the blue. When I least expect it, it grabs my awareness and lets its Presence be known. I get glimpses of it out of the corner of my eye. It is a fleeting knowing capturing my attention and bringing me into the moment. It sees me when nobody is watching.

All I have to do is crave the truth and it will make itself known.

*   *   *

Give Me Another Answer

Mentor Within, should I go study more shiatsu (a form of Japanese bodywork)?

Much of what has become known to you, is what you already have been called to do. Now there are ways in which you need to be taught that are beyond your current level of knowledge. I can teach you everything you need to know however, if you prefer to go this route. My love for you, Mary, supercedes any that any teacher of this world will ever have for you. You are God's grace in form and beauty. We will flow together like a wave in an ocean; are they indistinguishable?

I am stubborn and afraid so I ask the same question again.

Listen to what you are asking me. You are asking me for permission to go outside of yourself. What kind of Mentor Within would I be if I instructed you to go outside of yourself? You have already studied shiatsu and much more. Redoing is not necessary. Would you return to first grade and retake math class?

This is not the answer I want. It is much easier to find a mentor in the world than to have to go through this inner cycle. As uplifting and expansive as it can be, it can also be agonizing. It is not the way of the world. My Mentor Within will not give me a nicely printed certificate which I can hang on my wall as proof of my studies and accomplishment. How can I do anything without a certificate proving that I really know what I am doing? Who will believe me? Who will come?

Whoever is ready will come.

*   *   *

What if?

My boss calls this morning and wonders why I am not at work. Well, it is my day off! I feel guilty about calling her and saying I cannot come in today, that it is a scheduled day off. I am aware that I feel obligated to many things that other people do in this world that I really do not want to do. So I think that if I were a responsible person, I would go in to work on my day off.

It has to do with what this world calls our "identity." We are locked up in these ideas of who we are and what jobs to perform in order to maintain our identity. What if Jesus decided he was a carpenter first and foremost and though he had these inner movements to spend time meditating, sharing the truth, healing the sick and poor in spirit, but he felt obligated to do nothing but carpentry? No matter how strong the pull to listen within and follow, what if he chose to do the "responsible" thing and just stick with carpentry? After all, it is a reputable profession. Jesus was not motivated by the things of this world. He was not motivated by his identity in the world. He was motivated by love and living out the truth.

This is difficult for me to accept. A part of me feels irresponsible because I am not prompt about returning phone calls, emails, sending birthday greetings ... another endless list of worldly obligations.

*   *   *

There is Only One Need

Mary, let me ask you this. If you were walking along the road and a man who was bearded, wearing dirtied once-white clothing, the looks of a drifter, and no shoes, approached you and asked, "What have you done with my shoes?" would you frantically go looking for his shoes? No, because you are clueless as to the location of his shoes. Your search for his shoes would be fruitless, just as your search to satisfy other people's needs will be fruitless, particularly the frivolous "needs."

You are sensitive to the enormity of people's needs and it overwhelms you. They come to you with back pain, neck pain, shoulder pain, constipation, irritability, low self-worth, fear, headaches, loneliness, confusion, doubt … The list is endless.

Just as you would not search for this drifter's shoes, you do not need to search for the cure to everyone's ailments and fulfill their need for physical and/or emotional relief. You will be on a frantic, fruitless search because sickness is never ending. So when you are pressed to go to work on your day off or return endless phone calls and emails, you are basically feeling that someone is asking you to fulfill a need of his or hers and it overwhelms you. You cannot even fill your own needs. Most importantly, all of these requests, tugs, and obligations of the world really disturb you because you know the absurdity of all of it. You know there is only one need.

*   *   *

Suffering

People do not really want from you anyway what they appear to be asking. On some level they may want attention or relief from ailments, but your work is healing. Healing does not in any way imply that a person should get what he or she asks for or that you should get rid of his pain, return her phone call, make her happy, send emails …. This has nothing to do with healing. Jesus performed miracles because he was trying to connect with people on a level they could understand. Unfortunately, most of them still did not understand (and still do not) and they clung to this level and saw him as a sort of divine magician who could save them from their suffering.

People's real suffering comes from clinging to a life that has nothing to offer them — a life they were raised to pursue in order to "succeed" and "live happily ever after."

You have been called to this earth to address the need that most people do not even know they have. Your calling is to assist people along their journey. Imagine that you are simply God's helper. You stand at the doorway and put your hand out to assist each and every person. You take their arms to steady them like a "Boy Scout" helping an elderly woman up the curb.

I am sorry if it disappoints you that your job does not seem big enough. Actually, I am letting you off the hook and giving you permission to do just exactly what you know you really want to do, "Loving one person at a time and bringing people closer to God." You are such a great lover, so let yourself love!

*   *   *

What is the purpose of this book?

To share yourself with others. To become more of who you are. To shatter your own beliefs about mentors, that they must be individuals outside of you who have "made it" in the world, and about knowledge, that it can only be gained in academia, and about intuition, that it is a gift that is fleeting and cannot be trusted. Mary, the purpose is to claim God's gifts to you.

*   *   *

Never Forsaken

I fear so much following this Voice within. Why?

You fear that which you think belongs to you. I do not belong to you. I am not your possession that you have to defend and maintain a tight hold on. You fear losing our connection, and then where will you be? I cannot be lost. I will always be with you for you to call on.

I am afraid to follow a Voice that does not seem to be a voice of this world and that I will be called on to do unconventional ways that frighten me. I will be judged.

You will always be judged, whether you follow a traditional path or an unconventional path, because you live in a world of judgers. That is what human beings do: analyze, judge, evaluate. Humans love to do this. Mary, I do not come to frighten you. I know you crave security. I also know and so do you that no amount of money or worldly possessions makes you feel secure. You fear losing them, running out of them, losing the people, places, and jobs that provide this supposed security. You have been in "secure" scenarios and still felt like the rug would be pulled out from under you at any time. There is no peace in this place. In fact, you have many times in your life chosen the less "secure" route. You are a risk taker; you have left "secure" jobs, love relationships, friendships, and environments. You have withstood the judgment (inner and outer), you have faced the fear, you have been paralyzed with fear, you have clung to your breath refusing to end your time on this planet. Even when a frightened little voice told you it was time to give up and end it all, you chose life. You have already done the hard part.

Trust me, Mary. I know you find it hard to trust. But if you look back over your life, you will see that I have never let you down. People have let you down, but I have never forsaken you and I never will. I will not promise you with the lies of the world because I know you do not believe in these promises. Promises of the world make you anxious about your future. When you feel like you are getting hard on yourself and beating yourself up, you know you have lost contact with your Mentor Within and you are trying to do it alone.

*   *   *

Confidence

Mentor Within, I need something from you that I have not gotten from anybody else, any therapy of any kind. I need confidence to follow my intuition, to put myself out there in the world with the gifts I have been given. Can you give me confidence?

I do not think much of confidence, so no, I cannot give you confidence. Confidence is a human endeavor based on ego and hierarchy. So, if you are waiting for me to give you confidence, do not. Confidence waxes and wanes. It is only the confidence in God's plan for your life that I will honor you with, once this is what you truly desire. I am with you and it is this promise you may have confidence in.

So, how do I go out into the world and present myself to others without confidence?

Stop thinking of it as presenting yourself to others.

* * *

Quicksand

Mentor Within, I am down here in this world of fear, obstacles, stubbornness, resistance - all that - I am in the thick of it, in the quicksand. I need you to connect with me on my level. I really want to receive what you have to offer, but if it is too ethereal I cannot grasp it.

By the grace of God and your own free will, you can rise to this level. At some point, it is a choice. I can help you along the way with each and every choice, but you can choose to not listen and go your own way. I can lead you out of the quicksand. I can lead you out of your small mind, but from where I stand, there is no quicksand. It is all in your mind. If I were to join you at that level of fear, resistance, and obstacles, I would now be your earthly therapist. There are many earthly therapists available to you. There is only one Mentor Within.

* * *

Why Listen?

Who is the Mentor Within? Who are you?

I am that aspect of yourself that is grounded in a different reality, but I understand your world.

Why should I listen to you?

You cannot help but listen to me. I never asked you to listen. You know to listen.

I feel like you have volumes of information for me. What do you want to be the focus?

How you came to accept the Voice of the Mentor Within.

So, how can I come to accept the Mentor Within?

Continue to nurture your relationship with God.

I cannot stand waiting anymore and
at the same time, I cannot stop waiting.

Chapter Two: June

The work begins with you.

All that You Need

I am entering a time of a very private and personal relationship with you. I feel the presence of God very strongly. I am also feeling like I do not want to have to explain myself to anybody and this relationship that is brewing. I especially think of someone I know, who is so frozen in her concept of what a relationship with God looks like. She has a lot of rules. How do I handle people like her with their rules and mindsets?

Do not fear those who try to keep you within their fences. Their day will come when they will finally see the truth and all of their limitations will fall away. You must stand strong in your own experience and not be led astray.

I so want to immerse myself in the work.

You have a tremendous capacity to give. All that you need will be supplied.

*   *   *

The Work Begins with You

Great. Now, when can I get started?

I notice that as anxious as you are to begin the work, that you are also scared to begin.

I am scared. How are you going to help me with beginning this work? I am feeling you moving in very close right now. I feel that I am in close physical proximity to where I will be doing the work. Really close.

That is right. Because the work begins with you. You are your first client. I notice that you have tremendous resistance to doing this work on yourself. It can be done on yourself and really must begin here; the work will unfold within you. Let the Source speak through your own being. You may move, sit still,

do self-bodywork, but you are not to follow any previously written-down descriptions, rules, guidelines. Listen and follow these instructions. Eventually, you will be teaching people how to heal themselves.

I am wondering why I just had a memory of Gail, a woman from my Structural Bodywork Awareness studies. She died suddenly a couple of years ago. I do remember that she poured her heart and soul into her work. It was a time of real change in her life.

I hate to have to do self-work. It is so much harder because it requires such discipline and commitment. What time of day am I to do the work?

Morning is the best time. Your mind is quiet and time will not be spent just working off superficial tension.

How much time do I spend?

Thirty minutes.

Do I meditate?

This is your meditation.

I got home from work, meditated, and asked the Mentor Within about this self-work I am to do. I heard to go for a walk. It was cold and rainy, an unusual June day, but I went for a walk. My thoughts turned to John and our relationship.

Mentor Within, what have you to say of John and me?

Blessed be those whose love for one another is chosen by God.

I realized when walking this evening and felt my stiff neck, that I was focused on this self-work being me doing physical healings on myself. Then I thought, I do not think it is at the physical level that I am to focus. Is this true?

(No answer.)

*   *   *

I just got home from the hospital where I work as an occupational therapist and I am feeling kind of depressed. My back hurts. This work is really hard on my body. It is hard to participate in the narrowness of western medicine.

Mentor Within, what do I do? I want so much to break free of all of this. I feel like it is time for me to start living my life and doing what I want to do instead of what I have to do, or think I have to do. I could be teaching more classes, workshops, continuing education programs, movement, and doing more shiatsu. When do I finally just start? I am delaying moving forward with my life and feel like I am wasting time.

I paused here in my writing to do my daily meditation, which just so happened to include this scripture,

> *"They were all filled with the Holy Spirit and began to speak different languages as the Spirit gave them power to express themselves."*   Acts 2:4

This was my last week of Bridges, a meditation and contemplative "retreat in the world," which I have been doing for nine months on the spiritual exercises of St. Ignatius of Loyola. St. Ignatius, a Christian mystic, founded the Society of Jesus, the Jesuit order. I come out of meditation still feeling torn between my current work and moving more fully into that which I feel called.

About twenty years ago you were in a similar predicament. You have engaged in this internal warfare with yourself for twenty years.

I recall my work twenty years ago at a local hospital treating individuals with chemical dependency, eating disorder, and stress addictions, and a practicum I did as a graduate psychology student at a behavioral medicine clinic. I am sure this is the experience to which the Mentor refers.

You said you cannot give me "confidence" because this is something of the world and it waxes and wanes. I need something like confidence. How about courage? Can you provide me with what I need? At this moment, the telephone rang and an old friend asked me if I had any interest in renting studio space from him for my work. I thought this was interesting timing. Am I to rent this studio space for my work?

No. Put yourself in the position of one who rents space and you will pay a price. Your home is your office.

What will you provide me with which will give me the umpf and be the catalyst for me to finally start living what I believe?

Passion. Your passion and love will drive you. *Project Healing.*

What is *Project Healing*? I have this idea that it is a non-profit organization where volunteers go to nursing homes providing energy work, qigong, massage, movement. But this sounds like my idea, not necessarily your idea.

(No answer.)

*   *   *

I went for a walk in the rain last night. What do I do today? What about the pain in my back?

In addition to meeting with all of your clients, you are to meet with me in meditation. Let go of the agony. Feel it being absorbed out of the skeleton in your mind that foresees fear and danger.

I did this while lying in bed that night. I let the agony be taken from me. I went right to sleep which very seldom happens.

*   *   *

Stop Pretending

Today I showed a patient qigong and did some shiatsu on her and she was very receptive. She was able to walk 15 feet further, had decreased pain, and delayed her pain medication. What a blessing.

I am so exhausted from doing this hospital work; I cannot imagine how I will continue to "fit" myself into this bottleneck for two more months. What should I do?

Everything you want to do which you are not doing. You must begin full-time devotion to your efforts.

How do I give full-time devotion when I am working full-time?

You do not. Herein lays the problem. A master does not work part-time as something other than a master. You must use the resources available to you while they are available. Everyone recognizes your talents but you.

I recognize my talents. I am just afraid of not being provided for.

You will be provided for when you claim the truth of your existence, not a minute before.

What is the truth of my existence?

Right now you are stabbing yourself into a painful death. Acknowledge your Self and stop pretending that you do not know what I am talking about. Open the pages and start reading.

I cannot stand waiting anymore and at the same time I cannot stop waiting. I keep making new commitments to other things and the time keeps passing. Is there a way for me to integrate this healing work at the hospital?

Surely you realize how limited you are in this scenario.

Apparently I am not realizing much these days. I feel so depleted and so angry that I feel so depleted. I am not helping people at the hospital. Yes, we are connecting, my patients and I, and the connection is sweet, but most of the time is wasted hauling them around in their wheelchairs, transferring, or using the toilet. Some have a chance to "come back to life," while others are struggling to leave this earth and yet we make them cling to this miserable existence.

I feel like an alcoholic or food-oholic only I am not addicted to alcohol or food. I am addicted to insisting that the "world's way" is better than the truth I hear every minute of the day. I will not let go, no matter how insane, crazy, and miserable it all is, no matter how depleted and depressed I get. Like a drug addict on the streets, I keep going back for more. I am so angry. How far must I reach to hit bottom? My patient Louise is a godsend. She shares how at 59 years old and with loads of health problems, she has not lived her life. She lets herself be controlled by others who think they know what is best for her. She has been near death three times, but says, "God keeps sending me back."

I am not the kind of person who can do just a little bit of my passion as a hobby. I am an all or nothing person. Do it or don't do it. Otherwise, I feel fragmented, divided, confused, depleted, and like I am wasting my time. I work intensely, focused and purposeful, and though I can perform many tasks at once, I become much depleted. This world continues to not make any sense to me.

You may be finally getting it. Your running around at the hospital is not helping anybody. You have spent the last three months of your life thinking that you are providing a service that is "helping." Are you satisfied yet? There is a place and a time for that kind of work and even a person to do it, but you are not that person and it is not your place and time.

***Project Healing* specializes in providing nourishment, "food for the soul" for the person who is feeling depleted, ill, or having difficulty functioning. You will cater to the individual, incorporating modalities which will address their current state of "health." When one is able to surrender to the gift of healing that is offered to us by the Holy Spirit, Who is at one with Christ and is forever living within, one experiences health.**

What will I do?

You needed "confidence." I am giving you Louise, a woman to work with who will help you with your own self-healing; you will help each other. Part of you being your own first client is by doing your own healing with another person. It is too hard,

I can see, for you to do it alone. For you, teaching and healing are one in the same, healing yourself and others. Louise made it clear to you that she wants you to help her heal herself and she wants to help you. In Louise, I have given you what you need, not confidence, but a "healing connection." Louise is open, ready, and willing, unlike some others you may have chosen on your own who are not ready for the experiment.

Project Healing is "experimental therapy" so to speak, in that no two sessions are alike and I allow the Voice of healing to come through.

Thank you.

Unlock the door and anything is possible; keep the door locked and nothing is possible; throw away the key and you will never know. Persist. The addiction cannot be given up slowly. Give it all up to God or give up nothing. You do not need anything you have been doing for sustenance; let me sustain you. I cannot encourage you enough to stop doing what you are doing. You are starving your Self to death no matter how much you seem to be eating. It will never satisfy.

I feel like an alcoholic who promises to stop drinking tomorrow and wants so much to do so, but my "job" is to drink. That is what I get paid to do; that is what I committed to; I agreed to drink. I am going to let a lot of people down if I "stop drinking."

You are not responsible for saving anyone's ego.

I really do feel like an addict who is afraid to stop doing what I think is keeping me alive.

You are not afraid to stop "drinking," you are afraid of looking people in the eye and showing them the truth, because you want their support and you know they will think you are crazy and irresponsible, or they might think you are a genius, and then you are depriving them of witnessing a miracle. You are depriving everyone by living a lie. It is all a cover-up.

You are afraid everything I am saying is a crock and what if you need that job back and they will never hire you again. You know with all your heart and soul that you are not imagining any of this. I am real and you can be too. You have exhausted the possibilities, Mary.

Remember your dream last night. You were shown Life after the resurrection. You climbed a large stairway and at the top, you saw the Holy Trinity. Then you were sent back down the stairway and you began telling people that you just saw what happens after the resurrection — you get to be with God.

Remember the other day that I told you that your only job was to stand at the doorway (you envisioned a doorway at the bottom of a large stairway), and like a "Boy Scout" help each person up the first step; steadying them as they take that first step. Well, I gave you a look at what is at the top of that stairway and now I have sent you back down to begin your work. Take your post at the doorway, at the bottom of the stairs. Ready?

Yes, I am.

*   *   *

I am feeling really unsettled in this moment. As I surf the Internet and read articles about all the different types of bodywork techniques, I see that everyone is searching for healing. People want answers. They want relief. I am aware of my judgments of all the thousands of people I see out there teaching; a profession and holy endeavor that I do not take lightly. People just start teaching whether they have anything to teach or not or whether they even know how to teach. I have so much energy stored up inside of me for giving to others, I am ready to explode. I want to be the hospital in-house holistic healing therapist.

You can be anything you want.

I feel so laid back and anxious at the same time.

Let yourself feel the emptiness beneath it all.

*   *   *

On Display

I notice I keep wanting something to look forward to, to keep me pumped up and excited about living. This moment in and of itself feels so empty without a plan.

Mary, I will be with you whatever you plan. But do not be so busy making your own plans that you miss out on what really matters. You have the capacity to do some really "great" things in this world, according to the world; to be famous, to be known, and a part of you knows you can do it; you could be popular. So, that part of you which knows you "have what it takes" to be known and popular, fights with that part of you that relishes peace, quiet, and time just to cruise along your inner journey, and to travel the terrain within your own soul — what a vast world lies within. I know your struggle. It is like asking yourself to be able to remain in your cocoon exploring the inner life, while also on display like a dead butterfly propped up in a glass cage. That is no life for a butterfly. It is no wonder that you prefer the life of the cocoon. Outside seems like frozen tundra.

It is true. The outer life of this world does not seem nearly as exciting and rewarding as my inner life and relationship with solitude, with you, and with God. But, I am not a monk. I do live in this world. How am I to live in the outer world?

Invite others into your solitude. Bring others into a place where they may not otherwise venture. That is what you have to offer — the reality of something other than what others experience day in and day out as reality. People do not need more external, outer, worldly activities. They will come to you to go within. You will go within together. You will provide inner space for the inner journey. This is why no outer physical space or tangible business card, brochure, or marketing plan is clicking for you, because you are trying to create some outer image that will draw people to you. None of this "outer" stuff will ever feel right to you because it does not really matter. That is not what you are "selling," so

to speak. You are "selling" that which cannot in fact be sold because it is not tangible and it is unknown until it is known, and then that which lies beyond it is unknown. So, the more you think about where to do your work and what to put on your business card, the more frustrated you become. There is no physical space or business card that will ever symbolize that which you know to be true within. Everything in this world will fall short of your experience of the truth that lies within.

Okay, so where does that leave me? How do I do this work without bodies to work on?

Through meditation and qigong you are working on the world.

Yes, but what about bodywork?

Only for the sole purpose of leading people within.

So, the body is like the doorway at the bottom of the stairway and I am helping people through the doorway up on to that first step?

Your work is to take people on an inner journey. Your work is awakening others to the Spirit within, not physical therapy.

*   *   *

The Body

Why go through the body at all?

Because suffering is often experienced at the level of the body.

So, the physical touch and movement is a "way" to access that truth which lies within?

Yes. The truth that lies within Spirit. The key is for you to not get hung up on the physical, but to keep surrendering to Spirit. This is not emotional release work, though this may be a natural occurrence. Eventually, people will find stillness and know that it is not about the body.

So, this really changes things. My focus is not at all on relieving people's physical pain, though they may experience relief on a physical level.

Now do you realize why this has been such a struggle for you? You keep insisting that your work has to focus on physical "techniques" and have physical effects. But this is not your work. Your work is not grounded in the physical. It is grounded in the inner truth, in the spiritual. It just so happens that the form is physical.

This is such an immense relief that I am in shock. My personal experience has been that the physical forms of touch and movement have brought me into the Stillness. They have been such a significant part of my spiritual unfolding. I wanted to share the spiritual with others, but then I got locked up in the physical and lost my sight. It really is not about the physical. It is about awakening to the Spirit within. I have been trying to do the physical, to market the physical, but hide the whole purpose of it behind the curtain. Then I become perpetually frustrated because people just want to get rid of their physical pain and/or I have burdened myself with having to get rid of their physical pain.

My love is the inner journey of letting the truth show its Self to me while I happen to be engaging in touch or movement. This really changes things. This is a whole different path. An entirely different focus. I feel like I am coming out of the closet. I am coming out of hiding. No longer trying to sneak the truth, the spiritual, in the back door. I feel free now to tell it like it is. To be who I am. Not "physical" Mary of the world who uses techniques and has factual answers to address physical problems, but my true Self, who may use the physical as a means of expressing Spirit! Unbelievable. I am absolutely blown away.

To an outsider this may seem like a "no brainer," but to me it is the answer to a life-long struggle. It is permission to go within, to let the inner Voice speak and lead the way. No wonder I never felt drawn to go out into the world and do this, that, or the other thing. If I had to leave the wisdom of the Self behind in order to follow rules, protocols, and previously established methods, I just felt, "why bother?" I am happier on my solitary journey. Something has cracked open. I have accepted the physical for what it is: nothing, without back-up. Its only real purpose for me is to be a form to express the Spirit within and a doorway to access the truth within. I have gotten hung up on the physical level hoping that it would provide the answers, the solutions, the peace, the right space, the right business card, the right brochure, the right technique, more techniques .... The physical is simply a mode of transportation" and a "mode of expression," so to speak.

Today I fell into this moment of truth and saw the physical as really unnecessary in the overall plan, in spiritual healing. This felt a bit scary because I did not feel quite ready to let go of the physical. At the same time, I do not feel a need to be doing movement or bodywork in order to experience God. Stillness is resting in and all around me. It is at these times, amidst the Stillness beyond sensation, that I feel I do not need to come back to the physical world, but I do. For now, I do. So, here I Am.

No wonder that I have not been able to get "out there" in the world and do bodywork and movement. I have been keeping the most important aspect of the work to myself, the inner spiritual journey. No wonder it always seemed not quite it, to be dry, dull, boring. What is the point of doing the physical if one is not going to take the inner journey to awaken to the Spirit within; it is meaningless in and of itself. All of it. I am blown away by all of this. I feel set free.

*　　*　　*

The People Mover

My ministry is opening the door to the Mentor Within.

This work is not about preaching, evangelizing, or convincing someone to believe something. It is about leading people within so they can take the journey to the truth. All you have to do, is be.

It is like getting back on the "people mover," only now it is on its way back to Heaven. The "people mover" refers to a vision which came to me a few years ago.

I was driving to work early one morning and was so disturbed by the environment within which I had to work on this particular day. As an occupational therapist, I went to work two of the five days a week at a factory. This dungeon of a nightmare appeared to me as hopeless, God - forsaken territory. Why had I been sent here? Certainly not to teach injury prevention, as it appeared, because that wasn't working. The employees thought injury prevention was a real joke considering the work they had to perform. The employer had no real interest in injury prevention. I was just there because it looked good on paper to have a person teaching injury prevention and kept their worker's compensation premiums down.

The employees ran the gamut from beer drinkers, drug users, battered spouses, batterers, ordinary folks just trying to make a living, dulled minds, creative minds who found creative outlets outside of work, bible reading workers who always took the time to bless me, gentle people who always had a smile for me, and paranoid people who saw me as on the side of their employer and the insurance company. Whenever I entered that factory, I literally felt like I had just entered hell. To me, this was hell on earth.

As I got closer to the factory, I began to sob. The tears came so fully that I felt like I was in a car wash. I could hardly see beyond the hood of my car. For some reason I did not pull over. I was drawn up into a vision in which I remembered being back in Heaven and was shown how it is that any of us end up here on earth. There were many people in Heaven, some walking around, others standing around conversing. It was quite peaceful. I was standing alone and looking off into the not-so-far distance where something caught my attention. I saw a large people mover like at the airports. I was not clear where it would take me, but I was curious. I had a sense that checking out the people mover was being a bit mischievous, so I looked around to see if anyone was looking and noticed that no one was paying any attention. So, I got on the people mover. A part of me expected the heavenly beings to try to stop me, but to my surprise no one did. However, it was clear that they were aware of my move, but that it was my choice and no one would stop me. Apparently it was a common choice to leave Heaven; people did it everyday. As I traveled along the people mover, I felt myself growing further and further away from God. My memories of Heaven gradually began to fade. I tried my hardest to remember my Life back in Heaven, but without success. I had entered earth and at that point I had completely forgotten that I was ever even in Heaven. Oh my God, I thought, this is how we get here. Our curiosity and free will gets the best of us and before we know it we take one step onto the people mover and there is no turning back. At this point, I "came to" and realized I was driving, or really, that God was driving. The tears had continued to blind me and pour down my face throughout this entire vision. I knew it was a miracle that I had not had an accident. I felt graced to have gotten to return to Heaven and to realize that I have a choice: Heaven or hell.

As I entered the factory on this day, I realized that hell was in my mind. I walked out into the factory and instead of making my usual stops, I found myself walking nonstop around the entire plant singing songs of praise. The words fell spontaneously from my mouth. These were not songs I knew. They were being composed in the moment as I felt my Self blessing the entire factory and all of the people in it. I felt blessed. I was not in hell. I was with God.

Today I feel that I have finally been given the courage to be who I really am. Who am I, Mentor Within?

The custodian of truth.

Hallelujah! I am speechless. I drop to my knees and reach my outstretched arms to the ceiling. I have met Christ. Giving thanks, I say the "Our Father." I always have questioned the part of this prayer that is an add-on which says, "as we wait in joyful hope for the coming of our savior, Jesus Christ." Since I was a child I thought, what is everyone waiting for? Christ is here now. Today I know that Christ is here now. I feel taken up.

*   *   *

Doing qigong today really felt wonderful. It was exactly where I was, just moving energy. I am still dwelling in all that arose last evening during meditation. I can be free to present my Self to others and not hide behind some form. I can be outspoken and honest about the inner journey being primary. So, what is next?

What is next is the beginning of a whole new journey for you.

Yes, after realizing about the meaninglessness of the physical in and of itself, I feel baffled about where to go from here. I do not feel like some spiritual guru with some form of meditation or breathwork to teach. Here I am still stuck in the western world of physical healthcare that has forgotten the Spirit. Okay, I am being a little harsh. But how do I bring the realm of truth into all of this physical stuff? My formal education is rooted in the physical, mental, and emotional aspects. I do not want to keep the truth to my Self. I want to share it with others.

For what purpose?

I would like to make a living at it because it is work I believe in and enjoy. I would like to share it with others because it is what really matters.

What is "it" that you want to share with others?

To encourage them to take their own inner journey and to see how every physical experience in this world is an opportunity to go within and have a relationship with God.

Why is having a relationship with God so important to you?

It is the only thing that really fills me. Even in the emptiness, the times that I feel so alone, it is fuller than the offerings of the world. It helps me to tolerate the world better because I can put it in perspective and see it for what it is; how unimportant are the things I call "priorities."

Okay. Good answer.

*   *   *

Ridiculousness

I am feeling very out of sorts today, out of the groove and not at all looking forward to my work day tomorrow. I had very little time to myself today and I know that is part of the problem. After becoming aware of how I have been hiding my Self behind the physical, yet being expected to go to work tomorrow and make the physical the priority, not the spiritual, I am not feeling very happy. Mentor Within, any advice?

You have been placing tremendous limitations on yourself, which is why you are in this predicament in the first place. Your journey must become even more inward at this point in time.

This is very hard for me. I get caught up in all of the patient's physical needs at the hospital. Halfway into my lunch break, I am just washing my hands to start lunch. How do I change these patterns of excess and perfectionism?

You do not. What would you change them to? You have tried to change your behavior and it does not work, or changed it only for short periods of time and then you revert back to the old ways. It is just more misery. Let go of these limitations that you have placed on yourself. Excess and perfectionism are limitations. They are valued in your world, nonetheless they are profound limitations. You will not be happy with yourself by doing life according to how the world suggests, because to you that feels "less than," "imperfect," "not up to par," and "not good enough." It is a never ending, vicious cycle like the rat on the wheel.

So what do I do? I know what you say is true because I have been there and done that.

Unload the load.

I do not know how to unload the load.

Okay, what just happened is a perfect example of how your mind goes astray. You are sitting here writing and contemplating. Someone whom you know walks by while you are in the midst of

listening and you engage in conversation out of obligation or just to be socially polite. This is an example of excess. You just caused yourself more work because you did what seemed the "right" thing to do. Okay, some part of you sees the ridiculousness of some of the activities which patients are forced to engage in. The funny part is that the patients themselves see the ridiculousness of it, but still participate because that is what they are supposed to do, they guess. So, everybody sees the ridiculousness of the situation and continues to participate out of obligation or for whatever reason. It seems like the right thing to do.

Right. So how do I transform all of this ridiculousness?

Stop participating. Ridiculousness cannot be transformed. We are back to trying to change your behavior again.

What do you mean, stop participating?

It cannot be changed. Stop trying to change ridiculousness into more ridiculousness.

How do I stop participating? Leave the planet?

I do not think you are ready for this answer. Your place is not in this world, so to speak.

Is this me talking or you? Because I feel that my place is not in this world. But here I am in it up to my ears and I am so frustrated and you are not helping! What do you mean that my place is not in this world?

Remember what I told you? You are the "Boy Scout" helping the old woman up the curb; getting her off the street onto safe ground. Only you are the "spiritual Boy Scout." Your world is of the spiritual realm, not of the earthly realm. This should excite you, for it is your natural propensity. I am not asking you to go to law school. I am assisting you in taking on your proper duties. Be grateful, have fun. It is fun to be an angel. You are not subject to the laws of this world.

This is absurd. How am I to be in the world and simultaneously not be subject to the laws of this world? People are going to read this and think I have really gone off the deep end.

This opportunity is not offered only to you. It is a gracious offer to everyone. You have not been specially chosen. Everyone has been specially chosen.

This is starting to get really out there.

This does not mean that you have to start walking around looking like a hippie or a space cadet.

I do not know what to do with this.

Remember your patient Louise who said, "You are a god-send," after you did qigong and shiatsu with her? Why is it so hard to believe? She is also a godsend, to you.

This is all getting too weird.

There is nothing to be scared of.

Where does Jesus come in on all of this?

He comes in loving you and awaiting your return to Heaven.

This is starting to sound like some sort of science fiction novel or psychiatric case study.

What makes you think this world is so real? Because you have been told it is real. That is it. You were told this is it; maybe there is life after death, who knows, this is reality so deal with it. The nun in tenth grade who told you and your mother that you could not go through life changing your mind when you wanted to bow out of chorus and take business math, was your first clue that this world is insane. I remember you having this experience of how insane this world is. You sat there thinking, "Why can't I go through life changing my mind? You mean once I make a decision I have to stick with it no matter what just because that is some-how supposed to look better and get me further in this world than changing my mind? My mind is always changing." The absurdity of this world really hit you then, Mary, and it just keeps getting more and more absurd.

*   *   *

I have been feeling something moving through me since 4 p.m. when I got off work. It is 10 p.m. now. I let go today at work, no effort. What is going on within me?

Just sleep on it tonight. Tomorrow will show itself to you soon enough.

Thankfully, I got off of work early today. I was not built to do this get up at 6 a.m. and plunge into work routine. I do it well, but I feel depleted. Is this job really for me, Mentor Within? My life today feels purposeless. I know I had an "effect" on patients today. They were thankful for our connection and so was I. They expressed appreciation verbally and/or nonverbally that someone really reached out and touched them physically, emotionally, and spiritually. I sensed this very clearly. Why do I feel like this is such a sliver of what is really possible?

Yesterday and today I approached my work differently, letting Spirit guide. I was just as productive, only it all seemed less effortful, more flowing.

* * *

Do you remember your dream last night?

Yes. I was living in a big house with my mother and father. I heard a noise and from the end of the hallway, I peered into the living room. To my amazement, I saw a woman who was half physical body and half spirit. I could make out her form, but she was somewhat translucent like a spirit. It was clear that her name was "Ruby." I went to my mother and father and told them that I saw a ghost who was an old woman, and her name was Ruby. However, she had some semblance of a body. They did not seem surprised. Then Ruby came into the bedroom and offered each of us a glass of water. My mother and father, who were sitting up in bed, took the water and drank without hesitation. I was sitting between them and also took the glass, but I started to take a drink and stopped. How do I know where this water came from, I thought. Who is this Ruby character; maybe she poisoned the water. I decided that seemed ridiculous and drank half the glass of water and felt fine. Then there was a knock at the door and I opened the door. It was a man, a fireman. I could see the fire truck on the street with other firemen. He was checking on us. I told him all was fine. So, Mentor Within, I have my own ideas about this dream, but what is your interpretation?

Ruby is my birthstone, symbolizing my higher Self present at birth. At the moment of my baptism, my parents and I were all offered the Holy Spirit, as symbolized by the water. My parents freely partake of the "spiritual water," showing trust. I show a lack of trust in my higher Self, Ruby. Her purpose is serving "healing water" or "spiritual drink," the water of the Holy Spirit. I hesitate to trust my higher Self and drink of the holy water. How is this interpretation?

What is it about your interpretation that scares you?

It is pretty clear that I am lacking trust in my higher Self. If I trust, I will not be secure. Then I remember the firemen showing up - interesting, for firemen need water to do their job, just like I need the Holy Spirit to do my job. Firemen also represent protectors, saviors. They have come knocking at my door at the same time my higher Self shows up with the healing water, the Holy Spirit.

You have let fear restrict you from fully receiving the Holy Spirit. You are resisting letting your spiritual thirst be quenched. You drank only half the water. Ruby is an old, wise woman in your dream. Remember what your patient said to you today about your wisdom? Ruby is also a servant. She is serving the Holy Spirit.

What about that Ruby had a body, but I could see through it; she was translucent. She held a serving tray when I saw her from a distance in the living room.

The "living room." Ruby is present enough in the physical to do her job of serving the healing waters of the Holy Spirit.

I decided to go meditate. As I sat down to meditate, a storm was brewing. I began to read Acts 2:1-36. As I read, "when suddenly there came from the heavens, a sound as of a violent wind which filled the entire room in which they were sitting," my living room filled with lightning followed by a shaking, violent thunder. This continued for awhile and then the rains came. I felt as if I was experiencing what the apostles had experienced. Then I read, "and there appeared to them tongues as of fire." I remembered the firemen in my dream. Ah, my dream had two symbols of the Holy Spirit, water and fire. The storm grew more intense. The sky filled with lightning and my windows and walls clattered. I continued to meditate. A jolt so loud came that I jumped and immediately began saying the "Our Father." Then I remembered that in my dream when Ruby handed me the glass of water, I held up the glass as if offering it for blessing and I said the "Our Father." Then I drank the water. As I continued to meditate, I invited the Holy Spirit in and spoke the words, "I receive the Holy Spirit, I am willing to receive the Holy Spirit, I promise to speak of the Holy Spirit." Mentor Within, what does this all mean?

Perhaps you find all this a bit disconcerting. Your mind is going a mile a minute. I feel your frustration.

*   *   *

Free Will

Why does this all have to be so mysterious?

Let me speak to you of mystery. Jesus' real death was that of surrendering his will to God. He died to his own way and ideas. He pictured another world so powerfully in his mind that he joined with it. Once he surrendered to God, his real free will ensued. We humans do not really have free will how we speak of it. How can we? We are bound to life on this earth. Our only free choice is the choice for God. Free will is will that resides in the Holy Spirit.

You just said "we" humans. What do you mean, "we"?

I am a part of you. I am in your humanness. I am just not invested in your humanness.

How do I get "free" will? The real thing.

Each time you surrender to the Holy Spirit you get free will.

What if I do not surrender to the Holy Spirit?

You get nothing.

What good does "real" free will do for me?

It has the ability to listen and act accordingly. You are listening.

Am I acting accordingly?

Some of the time.

How can I act accordingly more of the time?

It is not about acting accordingly "more of the time."

What is it about then?

It is about being in accordance with the holy scriptures.

What holy scriptures?

The one being written.

I am writing holy scriptures?

You are the holy scriptures. You have been written by God.

So I am to be in accordance with my higher Self, the real me that God has written?

Yes. Then your life becomes a holy scripture. Herein lies "being in accordance with the holy scriptures."

Perhaps you can restate this so I am sure I understand.

Okay. Understand this. God's holy scripture comes to life through you. You are writing holy scripture each time you surrender your will to the Holy Spirit, to God, and let your life unfold accordingly. Hence, you will be living in accordance with the scriptures. That is what Jesus did. He surrendered and let his life unfold, and as he did so, his life became the holy scriptures. This is what makes the holy scriptures alive today. You are living, alive holy scripture.

This is not going to fly well with a lot of people. It sounds potentially blasphemous.

Blasphemy is claiming that God is dead by forging His work in our lives.

What do you mean, "forging His work in our lives"?

We sign our name to His work. We are God's work. You are not your own work of art. You are not your own creator. *God writes you.*

I imagine earthly scholars tearing this apart.

They cannot tear apart that which God has created. They can only tear apart that which they have made.

I feel like I am having a live experience of the truth instead of just reading about it, studying it, and philosophizing. God is coming to life for me. Each one of us is potentially walking holy scripture.

*   *   *

How am I saved?

Forgive your brothers and sisters in Christ.

What is forgiveness?

Forgiveness is how you live your life. Like a rat on a treadmill chasing after paper balls or like a saint who knows better.

How do you suggest I live my life?

In deep union with God.

How about practically? How do I make a living?

Nothing is more practical than deep union with God.

But what about making a living?

Frequent your local church.

What does this mean?

Perhaps your "living" lies within a church.

In what capacity?

Providing ministry to the sick.

Could this be the adult day care program that came into my mind the other day while I walked around Concordia Seminary grounds and contemplated use of the space for rent on a nearby street?

Capacity is limited in that space.

What church?

The Church of the Healing Waters.

Whose church is this?

Everyone's church.

What would happen there?

Love. Everyone would come just to be loved.

Where is the physical space?

You are the physical space. You travel to the people.

Oh, my God. I can't ... I can believe this is unfolding. A traveling healing center. Who pays me?

All those who are willing to be healed — the suffering, the dying, the sick, the fearful and the blessed, for all have been blessed and are now reuniting with their original blessing bestowed upon them at their creation. All who are willing to see the face of God who sustains them will once again befriend their Self and the love of God.

I remember the image of standing in the doorway and helping people up the first step. I do imagine though having an actual physical space.

You may feel overwhelmed by all the initial barriers of such an endeavor. You will reach more people if you go to them.

Wow. I feel so peaceful about all of this, it is flowing, like "healing waters."

*   *   *

How do I Know You?

Last night I was thinking about how I distinguish my voice from the Mentor Within; how do I know who is who? I felt that when something is my idea I get wildly excited and my energy soars. I jump up and down and feel like I have the answer; I have solved all of my problems. I am soaring high. I have the world in my hands. Then all of this excitement soon fizzles and I am right back to where I started.

This idea from the Mentor Within makes me feel a peaceful excitement. I am not jumping up and down. I feel content, peaceful, and excited to contemplate, investigate, and keep on listening for guidance. To take it one step at a time. To be shown the way. This is *Project Healing* mentioned by the Mentor last week.

That is what Ruby brought to me in my dream, "healing waters." Funny, at work today I was in a patient's room and written on the board was the name of her rehab tech. It was "Ruby." A gentle reminder to surrender.

I still wonder about further shiatsu studies.

I know you do. If it will ease your mind, do it.

*   *   *

Mentor Within, I had an amazing day. The mother of a 23-year-old patient with brain tumors has been observing me working with her son. I am taking the place of his regular occupational therapist. She requested of my boss that I be his regular therapist. She appreciated the way I connected with her son and the holistic approach.

Then another patient and I were talking about spirituality, life, therapy and so on, and she said, "Mary, you ought to write a book." I had not told her that I was in the midst of writing a book.

Later on at the end of the day I had an "accidental" conversation with the director of pastoral care and my boss. The pastoral care person asked me to do a presentation with her on spirituality in the work place and perhaps some other programs down the line. What a day!

What now, Mentor Within?

Meditate.

What kind of meditation?

Meditation on beauty. Go within. The beauty is there.

My students encourage me to pursue a full-time shiatsu practice and stop practicing traditional occupational therapy.

You already know what to do. Your role has been assigned, the position filled. The start date is coming soon.

Do I go to Chicago to attend the three weeks of shiatsu training?

I am not reasoning with you on this one. Almost all of the time you will disagree with me on something because you are still in training, still being mentored. You will normally have doubts, desires, more questions, but reasoning will not serve you. How is it that you can believe in a God so belonging to you and still be willing to forget the remainder of your unspoken life?

Tell me why you are drawn to this shiatsu program?

I want more training. I imagine having my own school.

Okay, so here we are again. What is it you are really wanting? Go to that gnawing in the pit of your stomach.

I want to be free from all of these limitations of the body — my mind that sets the limitations. I want to study qigong and Tai Chi with Justin. I want to meditate. I want to teach people to heal themselves through listening, movement, touch, and prayer-meditation.

What does this have to do with further studies? You may be postponing your mastery at another level. Meditate.

A prayer came to me:

> *"Connect me to your innermost Self,*
> *establish me in the presence of your Being,*
> *motivate me to know You."*

*   *   *

Return to the Garden

Mastery? What is mastery?

Becoming who you are.

Who am I?

A false teacher.

What? How is that? How am I a false teacher?

You are a gardener who does not garden. You have a garden.

Where is my garden?

Right where you left it.

Where did I leave it?

In God's hands.

I am reminded of a very difficult time in my life about 12 years ago, the disintegration of my marriage. What I thought was "holy intact" was in fact dismantling at full throttle. The pain was so intense that if I had to feel another fraction of it I was sure to die. Worse yet, I would not be lucky enough to die. Rather, I would have to live on this God-forsaken earth for the rest of my life with a broken heart. It was at this time, walking along the beach, that I gave my heart to God. I asked God to take my heart into His hands for safekeeping. My heart was so fragile and I was so broken, that I knew I could not take care of my heart anymore. Only God could provide the care and security my heart needed.

What do you mean that I am a gardener who does not garden?

You are afraid to get your hands into something that you do not know where it will lead.

How do I become a gardener who gardens?

Return to the garden.

And then what?

Return to the garden again.

Are you saying that I need to practice what I preach?

I am saying that none of us are gardening.

What is gardening? How will I know when I am gardening?

You will stop asking so many questions. You will be gardening.

*   *   *

On the Other Side of Fear

Am I to do bodywork at a local healing center?

This all makes you nervous, doesn't it? Why?

I do not know. I imagine living out life more fully and it scares the death out of me.

What is at the root of all of this fear?

It is so much safer for me to stay with traditional work.

Why?

These are fixed positions. I know my limitations, there are job descriptions. I am willing to move a notch or two out of these job descriptions, but any more than that gets into unknown territory. What if people do not like what I do?

Fear of the unknown. You have nothing to fear. You are scaring yourself. There is a part of you that does not know better; part of you that you do not know; an unknown part of you. This is the unknown that you are afraid of. It is not anything out there. It is within you. You are afraid of that within you that you do not know. You will always be afraid of the unknown until you get to know this "unknown within yourself." Who is this unknown Self?

The Stillness within. The Kingdom of Heaven that lies within. I am afraid of it — and in love with it.

Are you willing to get to know the Kingdom of Heaven that lies within? Mary, the whole purpose of you doing shiatsu, body-work, qigong, movement, writing this book, is to come to know the Spirit of God within you. It is not in and of itself the shiatsu, qigong, meditation. It is that your path into this Kingdom of Heaven that lies within, happens to be dance, movement, shiatsu, meditation. These are your gardens, these are your gifts. The real purpose of gifts is not really what others get out of them or think of them, but that they are the path to God. The irony is we were not given gifts just to make a living or share them with others, though these things may happen, but they are your way into the Kingdom of Heaven that lies within. Your gifts are for your journey. They will take you into this unknown part of yourself that you fear. You already know from experience there is nothing in this unknown aspect to fear. On the other side of fear is God.

*   *   *

A Reflection of What Lies Within

Gardening your garden means using your gifts. When people use their gifts and wind up very lost, it is because they have forgotten the real purpose of their gifts. Using your gifts makes the unknown known. Fear dissolves and herein lies the Kingdom of Heaven. Welcome Home.

Your focus on using your gifts must not be on those who are at the receiving end. The focus is on your journey into God. So you who seeks "the" spiritual path, you who put your relationship with God above all else, you who long to know God, now the question is, how badly do you want to know God? Badly enough to use the gifts given to you?

When you share your gifts, it excites others, inspires them, moves them, draws them to you because you draw them closer to God. They recognize something that is within them. You provide a reflection for the Kingdom of Heaven that lies within us all.

*   *   *

Witness to the Darkness

I feel so aggravated today. I do not want to do anything. I feel so out of sorts. I am becoming more and more sensitive to other people's energy and I am absorbing energy that I find to be negative. No, this is not true. I know that I am feeling all of this because I am being judgmental. I am becoming more and more sensitive to my judgment of others and I am becoming more distressed by how often I judge. I just stood in front of a tree and did qigong and this helped somewhat. I think I picked up a lot of negative energy when I hugged someone today. There I go again. Enough of that. I feel so lazy.

Mentor Within, is it possible for me to pick up negative energy?

The truth is that it is not possible for you to pick up negative energy unless you believe that it is possible. You may observe the actions of another and darken your mind along with them. You may be a witness to the darkness rather than the Light and feel the darkness expanding in your own mind.

*　　*　　*

Your Work

I just realized that after coming off of nine months of deep, extended daily meditation that I feel full and at the same time, I feel empty.

You are much too hard on yourself. You are expecting yourself to live fully in two worlds and that is a lot to expect.

What do you mean? My job and my spiritual pursuits are two different worlds?

Make sure you know the difference. Your job is a means to an end. Your spiritual pursuits are an end in and of themselves. Once you have reached this level it is very difficult to be in the world.

So where does that leave me?

To pursue the physical or the spiritual. Pursuing the spiritual does not mean that you will not still be immersed in the physical world, but it will be in a different way. Pursuing just the physical or trying to pursue both such as you are doing now, will cause tremendous grief.

What do you mean when you say to "pursue the spiritual"?

You have nothing to accomplish in this physical world, so stop trying. Your work is not where you are working now.

Where is my work?

Your work is in your own mind.

My mind feels in a weakened condition. How do I deal with this? I feel so negative and depressed.

I cannot help but to imagine that you know the answer.

I give up. There is my answer. I give up.

Remember where beginnings come from, God. It is never too late to begin again. The Source of your enrichment in these past days is always retrievable to you in prayer and meditation. I am not a solo act. I wait for you to reach to me. I wait for you to return. I give you consent to delve deeper now.

How do I delve deeper?

Keep turning to me.

*   *   *

I Am Who I Am Looking For

JoAnn, the director of pastoral care at the hospital, asked me what I experience you as and I could not really explain. I replied, "an aspect of God." Are you an aspect of God?

What does that mean? An aspect of God?

Well, you feel like a communication line between me and God. It is like you hear me and simultaneously speak for God.

I am the one who accompanied you so that you may take your place in this world.

What place is that?

A confirmed speaker for God. Someone has to speak up.

Speak up about what?

The purpose of this existence — to find God in the remotest of all areas and in the closest of hearts and everywhere in between. I am not hiding.

How do I speak up about this?

Very carefully. You are a role model now. Be careful where your mind goes. You are able to take others with you. Do not just go anywhere. Locate the truth in your mind, speak it, be a voice for God. Meditation is especially important during this time.

What programs do I start at St. Mary's?

What about shiatsu? Isn't that on your mind first?

Yes, it is on my mind. I cannot imagine all this traveling to New York. What do you think?

I don't think.

You "don't think?"

I am in the Mind of God and so are You.

Maybe I am just totally ready to finally let all that lays within me flow into another. I get excited when I think about practicing at the hospital. I am too excited to meditate. Now that the formal meditation program that I have been in for the last nine months is over, what shall my meditation practice be?

Form a working relationship with Christ.

How do I form a working relationship with Christ?

By resting in the presence of Christ.

Okay. I just spent forty minutes resting in the presence of Christ. Now what?

Start doing your work.

Okay. I am ready to write this email to this shiatsu teacher. Will you help me?

No.

Why not?

This is happening in your world. You will work it out. You do not need help with this.

I notice that I do not even want to write the email because I feel like I am asking for something that no one can give me. I know that I am asking for something that no one can give me. It is not really more shiatsu studies that I want.

What do you want?

I want to go study to have the experience, but I do not know why I am wanting this experience. I feel a deep craving that feels elusive. I cannot get a hold of it. I reach for it and there is nothing for me to hold on to. I feel right there in that place where what I want is something that I reach out for and I feel the Presence, but I cannot grab it. I sense the Presence, but I cannot hold it. What a strange experience I am having right now. It is not my bodily hands actually reaching out. I am experiencing a non-bodily aspect of myself reaching out and sensing a Presence close to me. So close, but so outside of myself. What am I experiencing? Ruby?

The work outside the body. You are not craving a bodily experience, but a transcendent experience.

I feel so still that movement and touch will just distract me. I sense a Presence around me.

The body cannot hold this.

I feel like if I move, though I have no desire to even get up, that it may be gone. But even as I write this, I realize "It" cannot be gone. There is nothing I can do that will cause It to leave me. I feel "protected," like I am surrounded. What is this?

What do you think it is?

The peace of God. The quiet reflection of my soul ... Christ. Whatever it is, it is very quiet ... stillness ... still waters. I am aware of the contrast between the activity of doing and this Stillness. Do you have anything to share?

Sharing is all I have been doing.

Yeah, okay, so here I am.

This morning I spoke with someone at the shiatsu school and told her that I was looking for something exceptional, to have a mentor, someone to study with who knows about listening and the art and spiritual practice of shiatsu. When I got off the phone, I realized, "I am the person I am looking for." I remember the Voice within from years ago as I sat in the college cafeteria questioning this insane reality, saying, "There will never be another you."

I recall the dream I had the other morning. I had prayed as I fell asleep the night before to be given clear guidance in my dreams about whether or not to go study more shiatsu. The following morning, just seconds before my alarm went off, I had this dream. A friend of mine, who is a massage therapist and student of oriental medicine, came to me in this dream. He held his hand over his heart and in a soft knowing, as he looked back over his life after years of study in the world, said, "It was inside of me all along." (This is a person who has studied a lot in the world.) The obnoxious music of the alarm clock came on. I immediately recalled the dream and said to myself, "No, this cannot be the answer to my prayer. There must be another dream yet to come." I refused to accept the very clear, direct answer I had been given. The next day I inquired about further shiatsu studies.

As I was getting out of my car, I saw all of my oriental medicine and shiatsu books sprawled all over. I walked through the door into my apartment. I realized that my teachers in this world will be my clients.

Jesus is my personal healer and teacher not of this world.

*   *   *

Beauty

I had a dream last night that I was in Italy. I came upon a big, beautiful church and walked through the wide doorway. As I entered, I saw a live band all around the altar. They were all playing guitar and people were singing and moving. The oddity is that they were playing "Day Tripper" by the Beatles. I took a seat in the pew and at the other end sat a handsome fellow with a reddish beard and mustache. I noticed he wore a wedding ring, so that was that. Then the band began to play "I've Got a Feeling," another tune by the Beatles. Everyone rose to their feet inspired and joyful, then they transitioned into another tune of an entirely different genre and we all sat as if to hear a sermon. A man stood up and began speaking about Korea. The crowd responded with a sigh as they did not want to get on this topic. Across the aisle and up a few pews from me sat my father, only unlike in real life, he had facial hair. He said in response to the speaker, "You do not know what Korea is like until you have really been there. Outside of the gates are statues." Then the man sitting down the pew from me stood up to leave. As he passed by me, I saw him as Asian, and he slid his hand just above the surface of my body from head to toe.

Then my father and I began climbing a wall leading to the roof of the church. I was ahead of my father and helping him up. I climbed through the white window onto the roof and helped pull my father through. We both stood on the roof of the church and looked around. The first thing I saw was the most beautiful pale pink roses I have ever seen. There were flowers everywhere. I was struck with looking at such intense beauty throughout the whole rooftop that I broke into tears and began to walk around the roof and said to myself, "I have to change my life." (There was an unspoken implication of moving to a foreign land.) Then I woke up. Mentor Within, what does this dream mean? I have to change my life?

Beyond promises are the inner motions of Heaven. I cannot relay to you the filled cup that is given to each one of us at the time of our creation. We are given many opportunities to relinquish our selves to God. This is the life change spoken of in your dream.

What does my father symbolize in the dream?

A voice in the crowd. Real purpose in life is assuming your position.

What do you mean?

Your father is correcting the person who speaks from the altar who is speaking about that which he has neither experience nor knowledge on any level. He blatantly tells the speaker that he does not know of what he is speaking.

Okay, so what does all of this mean for me?

The crowd reacts to the speaker with a sigh, "Oh, not this topic again." Symbolizing what people hear week after week in church. Within they have "got a feeling" stirring. Then the preacher stands up and speaks and brings the people down. Your father is "the voice of correction." Then you both begin your ascent out of the church and upward onto the roof and are taken up into unforeseen beauty.

*   *   *

When I have a client, how do I engage the Mentor Within?

Be still. Ask inner questions. Listen for the answer.

Do I ask the client to go within to her inner mentor?

No.

Why not?

Most will not be able to because of inner resistance.

What could I have done differently with the client I just saw?

Listen for her. She is not listening. Treat accordingly.

Will I continue to teach shiatsu?

You are clearly straight on your way towards a deeper teaching. Do not get scared about a life that you have become used to falling

by the wayside. Internal teaching is happening now. You may be called to preach in other areas.

Before you act, remember why so many have forgotten their role and lost their way. May the plans of God, allowing you true freedom, be carried forward.

I headed up the stairs to teach for the afternoon feeling completely depleted. I muttered a call for strength, "Holy Spirit help me, I relinquish my life to you."

The people who signed up for shiatsu sessions began to file in the room. I assigned each person to a student as I felt called. I sat on the stairs in the corner of the room and looked on. Then I had the following experience while observing the class:

As the students began, an inner peace came over me. I looked out onto the students and all I saw were the students now transformed into angels welcoming the clients. The students, who have transformed into angels, greeted the clients with gentleness and showed them a place of rest. They welcomed them with love, compassion, and calm. I sensed airy, light, and gentle. I sat amidst a place where they were being prepared to meet God. I was in Heaven and the students were angels helping spirits transition. All I sensed was beauty. Like my dream on the roof of the church. I felt like I was on the roof of that church communing with the roses. I sat in hands indistinguishable from Spirit.

*   *   *

I just searched the Internet and saw all the Asian bodywork studies happening everywhere but St. Louis — there is nothing here. Then I realize that I am in St. Louis precisely because the trainings I want are not offered here. It is a blessing in disguise. I would spend my life in school. I am beginning a patchwork approach. My immediate goal is to begin my healing work anywhere and everywhere. Mentor Within, what do you think?

You forgot to mention your book. Your choice to not study more shiatsu is a good one. You can learn more in Self study. Immerse yourself in lending a helping hand to others. Begin.

*   *   *

Making Peace with the Light

Thank you for listening to me and answering my questions with such great clarity. Thank you for the peace of Christ that I have been experiencing. Mentor Within, is this really a book being written?

Yes.

Who will read it?

You are the first reader.

Is it to be read by any others?

Fortunately, yes. Besides the original content and message there will be possibilities for reality expansion. Yes, reality expansion, among many who choose to read this book.

I am wondering about it being too personal?

"Personal" is a poor choice of words. "Universal" is being deemed appropriate.

What is "reality expansion"?

Surprisingly enough few people have been able to express "the way of God" in their lives. Not for lack of trying by a good many, but by being unable to forfeit the rights to their existence.

Unable to forfeit the rights to their existence?

Yes, you know. We get a jump start on life and we are off and running. Perhaps you will understand better if I put it this way. I am unable to interfere in someone's life without some permission from that person.

How will I give you permission to "interfere" in my life?

By keeping good records of our conversations.

What if someone does not know about "giving permission"?

Reward them for their innocence.

How do I reward them for their innocence?

Search their heart and a passage will be cleared.

How do I search their heart?

Without hesitation, moment to moment.

Yes, but I am curious what you mean by "search their heart."

No one is without light.

Okay, so once I find the light in their heart, what do I do?

Make peace with it.

Why do I need to make peace with the light in someone else's heart?

Because it is the same light within you. Make peace with your own light.

I am not at peace with the light in my heart, am I?

How could you be?

At this point I had a sense of another voice beginning to speak. Mentor Within, you speak as if you have been through the same thing I am going through. Did you once "leave" God and find the way home? Who is this speaking?

This is the voice of another who heard our conversation and tapped in. Someone once like you. A helper.

The following is an inner conversation with a helper:

What do you mean, helper, when you say, "How could you be?"

It was years later before I even realized what I had experienced. It all happened so quickly.

What was difficult about your first exposure to the light?

Accepting it.

Why was it difficult to accept?

It did not fit my life at the time. My mind was elsewhere, on other things. Like a line in a play, it foretold the whole story, like a line in a play.

What whole story?

Why we cannot live peacefully in this world. Why we some day have to come to grips with our own reality. We make a profit here that only resembles the fruits of our ancestors and we label this "accomplishment."

But this is the American dream. This is life. Some people would say, well, at least we are trying and being productive members of society.

Do not charm yourself.

Mentor Within, now this sounds like your Voice again. Am I right?

Yes.

Thank you, helper, but I do not like where this conversation is going. This is depressing. Mentor Within, what is the purpose of this conversation?

Accepting God is not easy. We stumble and fall many times before we are willing to stop picking ourselves up and starting over again.

Is not picking myself up part of being responsible?

Now you are starting to sound like Satan tempting Jesus in the desert. Sound familiar? Do not worry, Mary, all of your efforts have been forgiven.

Mentor Within, why do I feel so depleted? I have no energy. I am dragging my feet. Am I depressed?

It has really been a wild ride for you, Mary. Life has thrown you a few curves, but you are not depressed. You are not even depleted.

Then why have I no energy?

Go dance.

I danced and I did feel much better after dancing.

* * *

Counterfeiting

Okay, I feel exhausted again. What is this about?

We wonder about so many things in life.

Are you saying I should not be concerned about how fatigued I feel?

You really cannot be serious.

What does this mean?

Mary, have you considered the way you counterfeit yourself in the world?

How am I a counterfeit?

Look how energized you feel after doing healing work and dancing versus traditional occupational therapy.

Okay, this is not clicking. I feel like this is my thinking, not the Mentor Within.

Why does it have to be different? Your fatigue is from continuing to force yourself to be different from who you really are. You are radical and you are trying to "fit in." You actually do think like me, you are me, in reality there is no you and me. Continue thinking for yourself and pretending you think what I am telling you is too "out there" and all the fatigue in the world will set its eyes on you. It is easy for other people to "assimilate" because most do not know any better. It is exhausting for you to assimilate because you know better. It is like you are waiting until you get sick, hit bottom, to finally say, I cannot do this anymore. It is always, "oh, just another month or two" with you or "maybe with this work over here I will not have to disguise myself."

You are in the midst of a major spiritual Self-awareness break-through and, yes, it is exhausting to hold the dam back with your 120 pound body, that has no strength when it comes to spiritual matters. It is clueless as to how to deal with what you are going through and, yes, weak. The flesh is too weak to overcome the Spirit and that is exactly what is happening to you. You are not

depressed. Even if you weighed 320 pounds you would not have the strength, no matter how acute and discerning your intellect. You do not have the strength. Holy treasures are stronger than you. So, go ahead, wear yourself out. I will still be here.

This is not the first time in my life I have heard loud and clear that another path awaits me, but that I must cut the strings that bind me and begin this other path 100%. Not 58%, not 42%, not 89%. The two paths do not mix, like oil and water. But I need support for this. Money does not grow on trees.

You will be supported. What makes you think you cannot support yourself on this path?

I know I could, but there will be a transition time.

No, there is no transition time. Your "transition times" never end. This is your mistake. You get lost for months and years during these transition times. There is no direct path. You meander and drive yourself deeper into prison.

Okay, so how do I begin?

Go home.

*　　*　　*

Today while doing qigong with a patient at the hospital, I heard an inner Voice speak, "Your patients will only be able to be healed to the extent that you are willing to be healed." I knew this referred to more of a spiritual healing, "opening to God," than a physical healing, though not excluding the physical. This was a real eye opener for me. I realized how important it is that I be open to my own healing.

I am so much more energized by doing healing work than traditional occupational therapy. Is this because I am releasing the limits on myself?

Anything that you feel limited by will exhaust you. The truth will set you free, and any way that you succumb to what you know to be not true will exhaust you.

I am hungry. Everything feels heavy and hard to digest. What should I be eating?

No matter what you eat there will always be hunger. Diet is not a priority. Just keep meditating.

Oh, to Heaven with it.

Chapter
Three: July

Find the pause.

Behind Every Face

Mentor Within, what would you have me do today?

See the truth within.

The chaplain at the hospital asked me today what are my "wildest dreams" in regards to my work at the hospital. I seek the truth only, no one's voice, but God's.

The truth seeks you.

What is my work at the hospital?

Letting the Spirit of God move through you. Joining is healing. Let your Self speak.

How do I do this?

We really must begin at the beginning. Since you began this path, much has happened to create great strides. The bittersweet has been alleviated. The tastes of the world keep you bound in a cycle, just as night gives way to day and day gives way to night. How come you still experience the bittersweet of life, you ask?

Yes, I do ask.

You experience the bittersweet in direct proportion to your beliefs about love. You believe and have experienced love as bittersweet.

Jesus was love and he drank from the bittersweet cup.

The bittersweet taste in Jesus' mouth was alleviated when he could no longer bear witness to the false mind and he surrendered to Love which transcends the bittersweet taste of your world. He became one with Love. Christ *is* Love. You have also struggled with the bittersweet of the world and have attempted to contain it, suppress it, and run from it, only to find your release in the moment of surrender.

So, how does surrender alleviate the bittersweet taste of the world.

It opens the door to that which lies beyond it — Christ, in whom there is no bittersweet.

How do I address people at the hospital?

Let the fruits of the season behold you.

What does this mean?

Behind every face lies the face of God. Enjoy the Spirit of the moment, belong to Christ and Christ will make clear your path. This is all much easier than you imagine. You worry yourself for no reason.

*   *   *

The Edge of Choice

I realized today that I stand on an edge. I can choose this ground that seems safe and stable and at the same time restraining, sabotaging and exhausting, or I can choose to surrender all the petty details of life to Christ. I am reminded of all the dreams that I have had where I am standing at the edge of a cliff and begin to fall off the edge and then I wake up. A common dream I know, but this is what I am feeling now. I am realizing that I have a choice every moment. To choose my world when I feel burdened with comforts and discomforts or just say, "Oh, to Heaven with it."

Many of my behaviors simply get in the way of the flow of life and get me caught up in a web of burdens. I am ready to unload. I realize that I only have to unload moment by moment. I have reached a point where it seems that my way is just getting in the way. I realize how much my way gets in God's way.

My work requires a willingness to be led, to surrender my will in exchange for God's Will. "I" have all kinds of ideas based on my training, upbringing, experience, beliefs, and values about how interacting with patients and coworkers "should" look. They have turned into dead rules and stagnant guidelines. They have no life. God is alive not dead. We can have simple exchanges of communication that bring life and vitality.

How will I get paid for this?

People will rejoice.

*   *   *

Judgment

Mentor Within, am I to do something with this whole concept of each of us having a "Mentor Within" besides writing a book? Like giving workshops, talks ... ?

The concept of each one of us having a "Mentor Within" is perhaps an idyllic view of the world to some people, but it is in fact very practical and useful in daily life. To share this experience with others will be a task in which all will be strengthened in their ability to listen without judgment. Notice I have just introduced a new concept, "judgment." The Mentor Within listens without judgment.

How does this help me?

You are constantly judging others and situations. This creates great anxiety in your world. What a hopeless method of existence, though you cherish it so.

I noticed today while practicing qigong that a part of me wanted to sink into a dark place. I was aware of the pull and how easy it would be to go there, this place that creates anxiety. Then I chose not to go there. I could feel all the judgments about myself rising up in this place. What can I do about this?

What did you do?

I surrendered. I asked that this place of depression and anxiety be taken from me.

And what happened?

I continued on with my practice more freed up.

*   *   *

Give Love Away

Rigorous discipline is what it takes to transform your life.

What kind of discipline?

Surrendering your will to God.

I am afraid that you have nothing more to tell me. Sometimes I am just afraid to live my life. I still need your help.

There is no reason to push your self. Yet your anxiety is coming from sitting with all this and trying to hold on to it until a certain time, until it is all perfectly understood and "packaged." The sooner you let go of all you are receiving, your anxiety will lessen. This is too much to hold.

Yes, it feels like when I was a student and had a paper to write. The longer I procrastinated the higher my anxiety. Once I got to work my anxiety lessened; energy was released. Is this what you mean?

You are getting exhausted because you are putting forth a lot of effort attempting to hold on to all that you are supposed to be letting go of. Give it away. More will come.

How do I give it away? I am wondering about getting a service trademark for the "Mentor Within."

Well, you cannot exactly trademark God. All you are doing — we are doing — is setting the record straight. You cannot protect this information, Mary. You cannot get a copyright on love. This is a new theme on an ancient idea. Christ never died. Christ lives within each and every one of us.

How do I present it to people? How do I give it away?

No particular method is suggested. Spontaneity is your strength.

What is my overall message if I am to get a service trademark on the Mentor Within?

The Mentor Within, who I Am, in reality cannot be trademarked.

What about helping people to contact the Mentor Within through movement and journaling?

You have received this information by the grace of God. It is your willingness to receive it and your thirst for the truth that has saved you.

So how can I be helpful to others along these lines?

Listen and keep writing.

*   *   *

The Unspoken Question

I wonder why I receive all this incredible information from you and then I go on living my life and interacting with others as if I haven't. I have changed my behavior and outlook somewhat, but I still get pulled into the world's desire for me and my desire to please the world, to live up to the world's expectations and interact with people in an habitual "appropriate" manner.

Often people speak to me or ask a question and they expect an appropriate response. They want to know they have been heard, they want empathy, they want guidance, they want answers. Most of the time if I go inside and ask Spirit for help, the answer I get is to remain silent or to send the question back to them so they can go within and find the answer. God does not give me a "socially-culturally appropriate" response.

When it happens to be that you currently find someone full of questions, resolve their business for them by answering the unspoken question; that will give them great freedom within.

What is the unspoken question?

Who am I? This is the root cause of anxiety that maintains the wheel of questions and the flipping through the potential responses to the questions.

I am imagining a game where a stack of cards is full of "answers" to questions and all my mind does is reach for the next "answer" - the top card on the stack. I realize the limits of my answers. Like this morning, I was meditating on Christ and my mind floated to the beach house we were considering staying at on vacation. Eventually I found myself saying "beach house" like a mantra. This mind is completely distractible. I had to laugh at myself.

What is the answer to this unspoken question, "Who am I"?

A crowd of masters gathered around to ponder the question, "Who am I"? While they were pondering, Christ walked in and poured each of them a glass of water. He rested the still full pitcher on the risen stone centered between them. Each drank from their own cup until each cup was emptied. They continued to ponder the question. All the while, Christ continued to reappear and fill their cups. Not one noticed from where their full cup came or the pitcher on the risen stone amidst them which remained full. Once again the door opened and Christ walked among them and filled their cups. This time one of the masters took notice of the servant and asked, "Who are you"? The servant replied, "I am Christ," and continued filling their cups.

*   *   *

Pause

What can I do to stop giving habitual, informational responses to people's comments and questions instead of saying what I know to be the truth or just remaining silent when I feel drawn to be silent. I want to put this information you are giving me to use. I do not want to ignore it.

Find the pause. You always have a pause. You always have this part of you that says, "Okay, you are drifting toward some response now that will make you look helpful, smart, concerned, like you know a lot, like you are being a good person ..." I know you hear this Voice loud and clear within you before you ever open your mouth. Agree?

Yes, I do want to look smart, helpful, impressive, socially appropriate, empathetic — all of this stuff.

When you stop wanting to look "socially appropriate" you will stop talking nonsense.

I cannot wear wrinkled clothes much less stop saying things that sound "appropriate" or "helpful." I am so caught up in appearance in that way and I hate it. It zaps my energy.

Well, apparently you do not hate it enough. You love your self more than God.

That is it, isn't it? That is really what it comes down to. I love myself and my ideas more than God. That is right! So, how do I come to love God more than myself?

This is the question. Render your self incomplete. Follow God even into the wind. Accept nothing but the truth. Together we came into the world, together we leave.

*   *   *

Spiritual Rehabilitation

I am concerned about my lack of motivation to initiate any work. I need a jumpstart. What do you suggest?

Mirror the wisdom of fellow human beings who have traveled toward God. We cannot lead ourselves into anything but darkness.

How do I mirror this wisdom?

Being fruitful in the eyes of God. Bear witness to your departure from the world. Cast aside your ways and leave behind the trails of disillusionment. Focus your life on serving others. Fear not what comes before you in anything you do. Just beginning your service will cast aside the tiredness that is so wearisome. Your teaching comes through service, through spiritual rehabilitation.

What is my purpose at the hospital?

To surrender the purpose of rehabilitation to God. All of these creatures are wandering around, patients, doctors, nurses, therapists; all searching for fulfillment. Masses come to be healed through surgery, drugs, and therapy, and some "healing" does occur, only nothing permanent. It is all quite temporary; fix-it, repair-it, replace-it, break-it, open-it, close-it, monitor-it ...

What is "spiritual rehabilitation?"

Excavating the Will of God which exists within each and every one of us.

Monitoring the progress of one's soul.

Landscaping the heart.

Seeking God within.

Relinquishing our minds to God.

Everyday.

Wow, this is a tall order.

Nothing matters except this.

I see five statements here, activities to be practiced daily. These are like the activities of daily living that we work on in occupational therapy, only these are spiritual activities. Where do I begin? Can we take one at a time?

Excavating the Will of God. **This is done through proper meditation.**

What is proper meditation?

Facing Christ in silence. Letting God's Will surface. You may feel underwater, yet breathe in the Holy Spirit, then let go of all that troubles you. Tears of joy may come, or laughter, release, love. Nothing matters. Fear is mine. All will be healed.

I cannot imagine anything more wondrous than this.

Monitoring the progress of one's soul. **It does not matter how far one travels on the spiritual journey. We have arrived each time we accept the mind of God.**

So what is there to monitor?

The level of one's participation in acceptance.

How do I accept the mind of God?

Bear witness.

How do I bear witness?

Let your Self be seen.

What is my "Self"?

You have been created in the image of God. Contemplate how aware you really are as one created in God's image.

How do I let my Self be seen?

Behold the womb of God. Dance away the darkness and feast on the Light of God. Meditate on Christ. Dance with the Holy Spirit. Pure awareness rises — your eyes rest upon Him — and then, you are seen.

Thank you.

Landscaping the heart. **Fertile soil awaits your feet. Christ walked the earth and the trees arranged themselves around him.**

What do you mean? Are you referring to Jesus?

Today we talk about facing the Christ within each and every one of us, and as we do, our eyes transform. We look beyond the humanness and seek the Christ within each person we encounter. Jesus allowed his walk to be with Christ. It is Christ who carried Jesus on this earth.

So, as a part of "spiritual rehabilitation," how do I landscape the heart?

As a messenger of God, your walk will be leading others, including yourself, to the doorways of Christ's heart — this is your mission. Through clear determination, seeing, and arranging yourself in relationship to God.

What do you mean by the "doorways of Christ's heart"?

Divine nature reveals itself in Christ. Christ is revealed in infinite Love. Love is revealed through you. Every step is away from God or toward God. Holy Spirit will open the doors. We enter, or not. Hence, the landscaping of the heart.

How do I go about "seeking God within"?

Seeking God within. You come across many different religions and belief systems, but seeking God within has little to do with these value systems and goals. In order to heal one's inner spiritual decay, one must have a desire to be healed. Recognizing our inner fragmentation is what eventually leads us to God; nothing in the world will make us feel whole again. We all have different levels of unhappiness that we are willing to tolerate. Reasoning and bargaining with God seems to get us nowhere. Building a bigger and better plan of our own has limits. Settling for struggle in life cultivates worn out ideas that dull the mind. Being capable of tolerating unhappiness is the best way to push away God. No desire to be healed can come from this mind set. So, when you are no longer capable of tolerating the unhappiness in yourself and the world, you will naturally seek God within, if you desire healing.

So seeking God within is a process one must come to upon surrendering one's unhappiness and brokenness to God, no matter how small, no matter how large. We have to want to know God.

What is the "soul"?

It is the river of your life. Our soul is our path in life. We unwind down the river towards God from beginning to end, but often we fear the "end" that spills into waters much larger than us or our small self. So often we mislead ourselves and our purpose here gets lost. Our souls drown in our own tears, yet all the while, God's hand, like a boat, is keeping us afloat on a level that we often are not aware of, but it is happening. We are saved from our self when we recognize and give way to the hand of God; salvation is near. Fear the nature of God and you will be trapped by your own convictions and blinded by your foresight.

Ignoring our purpose in life causes one to be led in directions away from one's primary Source. Spirit within does not decay, rather we rely on ourselves instead of God. Instead of growing in love, we grow in the direction of pain.

So, the next step of spiritual rehabilitation is "relinquishing our minds to God."

Relinquishing our minds to God is letting ourselves be persuaded that nothing matters but God's plan.

Lastly, spiritual rehabilitation is to be done everyday. Do you have anything to say about this daily practice?

How come, do you think, we need a daily practice of spiritual rehabilitation?

Because I am such a creature of bad habits that it is hard to undo these bad habits and I need a lot of practice.

Wrong. This is not about undoing bad habits. It is about cultivating a sincere sense of who you really are. Bad habits are for psychologists to help you work out. Do not waste your time on trying to change your behavior.

*   *   *

A Friend is

Mentor Within, today is my birthday. Do you have any special words for me today?

Friends are few and far between. A friend is not someone who binds your heart and strangles your voice. A friend is someone who mirrors back to you the wisdom of Christ. We, your spiritual friends, are not mentioned often in this book. We may not be with you in the body, we are with you in Spirit. Most people are clueless as to what "real friend" means. There is a magnitude of kindness required for perfect friendship. We have defined friendship in this culture as "love the way I want it." "Love the way I want it" is not friendship. Love the way God wants it is friendship. Rely on God as your best Friend. One who mentions their "requirements" for friendship has forgotten one's role in relationships. No one has the strength to come between you and God. Our relationship is not in need of forgiveness because there is only "One in you and you in One." Most every time you radiate perfection, I will be seen. Nothing matters but this; I am to be seen in the world.

*   *   *

Who's Who?

Mentor Within, you often refer to "Christ." Who is Christ?

Christ reigns in the realm of deliverance. He delivers us from our belief that we are nothing. It is this belief that haunts us until our death and even thereafter.

How does it haunt us?

Like a shadow following us down the street on a dark night. We sense its presence. It causes us to play little games with our minds to try and trick it away. We dash this way and that trying to dodge its hovering over us.

How do we receive deliverance from this belief?

Come to know thy one Self; Christ is within.

As I was walking in the rain, I asked, "What am I to do?" It seems that everything is falling away. So many practices I do or want to do are no longer meaningful, so what is the point. They are not the way to God. What did Jesus do, how did he walk this earth?

He allowed himself to be a vessel of the Holy Spirit. If people knew how Jesus really lived, some of the very people who profess to be Christians would proclaim him a sinner and be the ones to crucify him if he walked this earth today.

This struck me like lightning; how true I knew this to be. Jesus was radical, not radical for sake of rebellion, but radical for the sake of truth. Why would they proclaim him a sinner and crucify him?

They could not understand themselves and their reaction. He would portray a life outside of their familiar mind. Life offered through him would be otherwise.

Otherwise?

Without conviction in the possession of selfhood.

Doesn't one need a good sense of selfhood before one can recognize its faulty system and surrender to God's Will?

A trap of the false mind this is. God will guide your every action.

Who was Jesus?

Jesus was a man who gave himself to the truth because he saw no other way to God. He became lost in the ways of the world. He saw the lost world. He gave away his plans for the sake of finding God; he found God. Yesterday and tomorrow were not enough for him.

Is Jesus the Christ?

Many people believe him to be the Christ, but only a few have surrendered their thoughts about themselves to God, enough to know the Self, to know the Christ. Jesus did just that.

Most among you have forgotten Christ, or "I Am" is not good enough for you, so you believe in something or someone else. I am not magic. I am not your magician. I am the real you. You cannot live in the turmoil of your own mind and experience the Christ within. I see you waiting for me to come to you, but it is you that comes to me. I wait for you; I see you waiting and wondering.

So, Jesus went to you; he went to Christ within. He recognized you and stopped waiting.

Jesus had a long history of searching the world for the Light, and eventually Jesus gladly accepted the Christ within.

He did say, "the Kingdom of Heaven is within." Are we to worship Jesus as our savior from our sins?

Jesus saved himself; he turned his life over to God. He knew no other way to freedom. Christ is the reason for your salvation.

Who is the Holy Spirit?

The Healer within you.

What was the resurrection?

Jesus resurrected the moment he recognized the Christ within fully.

So he stayed in his body after the resurrection?

It was not until the moment of his death that he fully surrendered to God. He fully realized Christ as he breathed his last breath. The resurrection was a series of choices Jesus made to survive in the world. Jesus allowed the death of his self, choosing to be joined with Christ. At his death he saw the Holy Spirit descend upon him and alter his existence, taking him away into the realm of Spirit, out of the body and into the Light. Forsaken no more.

I am realizing that everything on this earth is meaningless, just as I am experiencing. This is my sign to surrender to the Christ within. To stop waiting for Christ, but to turn to Him and say, "Take this from me; take my hands, my heart, my spirit, my intentions." I am reminded of the song:

> *Into your hands, I commend my spirit, O Lord.*
>
> *Into your hands, we commend our love.*
>
> *For we must die to ourselves in loving you.*
>
> *Into your hands we commend our love.*

*　　*　　*

Nothing Matters But This

I am looking back on my notes as to what work I want to do at the hospital. I see all of the ideas and now I am not so sure. Now it just seems like a bunch of ideas. I felt that you were encouraging me at the time to pursue these ideas, but now I am thinking that I was encouraging myself and just had my mind set on what I wanted to do.

You are constantly being led in a new direction. I am watching you unfold. Do not let a commitment to some idea get you stuck on your path.

What keeps coming to my mind is, how do I speak about any of this to people. When I think of words, they sound corny and out of context, out of left field, unless I am already in a conversation about spirituality with someone. How do I share this with others? What does it look like?

Forgiveness is in the eyes of the beholder.

What does this mean?

You will know it when you see it. Let your self come to God.

This seems too elusive. I feel left up in the air, undone.

Talking about something that has not happened yet will do that to you.

Okay, so I am to begin by sharing this all with the chaplain at the hospital?

Yes.

Another step of spiritual rehabilitation is relinquishing our minds to God. It seems like we have talked a lot about this, but for clarification, what is relinquishing our minds to God?

Letting ourselves be persuaded that nothing matters, but God's plan.

I find that I often "forget" to relinquish my mind until I am deep in to my own mind.

Eventually, you will remember.

*   *   *

What is "sin"?

Managing our own time on this earth. Not trusting in the higher Voice within. Pretending not to see life for the gift it is.

Did Jesus die for my sins?

Jesus died because he was human. He traded his love for the world for the love of Christ within him. In so doing, he aggravated a lot of people who eventually decided to deal with their aggravation by getting rid of Jesus.

*   *   *

When is a good time to meditate?

Bed time.

I am thinking about doing the lessons of *A Course in Miracles* to help get focused. What do you think?

I shall remember a past time which you have since forgotten, that you did perform these lessons daily and they were of great help to you.

When was this past time?

It does not matter now.

Will they be of help to me now?

Only if you desire.

What purpose do they serve?

Relinquishing our minds to God, if we so desire.

I think a few years ago I did up to lesson eighty-something. Do you suggest I begin with lesson one?

Whatever causes you the least strain.

I do feel very close to Jesus. I always have. I feel such beauty when I imagine him.

Go to the Christ within and let your walk lay beauty on to other's eyes. Bless you, my child, for loving so.

This is starting to sound less like work and more like fun.

* * *

Mentor Within, it has been a long time since we have spoken. I am at this qigong workshop and love the idea of getting up early in the morning to practice, but the first thing I think of is needing to see my first patient at 7:30 a.m. I am just not a morning person!

Remain safe in God's hands. No problems will arise, as has been foreseen. Truth has completed itself in you and will never alarm you. It is as if love makes itself known to you the moment forgiveness happens. Seek willows and you will find trees — seek God and God will find you.

How do I find the discipline to awake so early to practice qigong?

You do not find the discipline. The discipline finds you. At what level would you like to be disciplined?

I would like to wake up early and practice at 6 a.m., but the alarm goes off and I refuse to get out of bed.

What is your real question?

What do you mean, "the discipline finds me"?

The discipline of God is found in the heart of one who grows weary of their own tactics, their own behavior.

What is meant by "level" of discipline and why did you ask me this?

The extent to which you are willing to cast your doubts into the water never to be seen again. How can I help with this?

Remove my doubts about my ability to get up early and practice qigong.

You clearly, in your mind, have a need to practice qigong.

Will you remove my doubts?

Will you circle the globe for the first hint of spring?

What do you mean?

Doubt is formed from lack of trust. Doubt is removed when Christ becomes your priority, the One in Whom you trust.

You are implying that I lack the initiative to make Christ my priority. The "first hint of spring" refers to Christ. What does "circle the globe" mean?

This is how hard it may seem.

Is qigong something you want me to practice?

Practice, "Will you be my healer."

What is "Will you be my healer"?

Your meditation on Christ.

*　　　*　　　*

Just Ask

I let the Mentor Within handle the mix-up with my computer software yesterday and today. I asked for practical help in the moment and received it! The salesperson who installed the software was fascinated with my book and wants to read it. All is well. Thank you.

* * *

Laughing at the Ego

I have noticed in the past 24 hours how I feel myself experiencing peace and at every turn something happens that could potentially disturb this peace. I have a momentary reaction and then I realize, "Oh no, ego, you are not as strong as the peace of Stillness," and I just laugh. Many of these upsetting things are quite minute and I see how I let myself blow them out of proportion.

* * *

Creatures of Habit

Mentor Within, I feel it is exhausting to live two lives. First, there is this earthly existence which involves maintaining a schedule, keeping up with the practicalities of life, having to be human, and do what it takes just for basic survival on this planet. Then there is this aspect of myself that just wants to meditate, pray, write, practice qigong and shiatsu, be in nature, stare at the trees and the sky, and just be with God. I find such peace here. Then I have to be "on" to go teach.

Please remind your students of the limited capacity of this world, of the grand scheme we have been participating in, of how we do not belong to this world. We belong to God.

I feel like a fraud when I teach because I do not believe in all of these theories. I feel so detached from all of the "facts."

Many observations are being made.

It is not that I "believe" in shiatsu. When I touch people I connect to a Higher Source that knows something that I do not. I am encouraged to listen because I hear a "knowing" that I cannot explain. I sense a connection to the One that knows and I am drawn deeper. It is not about theories; it is about touch, presence, listening, opening, and entering.

I found myself tonight repeating this absolutely stupid statement that I heard someone make awhile back, "People do not change. A person's personality is basically set by the time they are 26 and not much changes after that." I repeat this statement as if it is the God - sent truth. It is true, I guess, that personalities may not change much, but the person who made this remark implied that change is not possible after 26. I have changed a lot since I was 26. My point is, that I repeat these kinds of statements and I am back to being a fraud, or sometimes I feel "programmed." I just say and do certain things and afterwards say, "What was that, who was that?" Why do I do this? I am not letting the real me be seen. I hate when I behave in this manner. What is the underlying fear that causes me to perpetuate my false self?

"Habit," by its nature, repeats itself. Stress encourages habit. By nature humans seek repetitive motion, both mental and physical.

How can I stop this behavior?

Step back from the mental confusion.

*   *   *

God Wants to Talk to You

I had this incredible dream this morning. Everywhere I wanted to go there were snakes underground, just beneath the surface. I wanted to walk through this arched doorway that was outside in the midst of nature. Someone began yelling to warn me about the snakes. I got scared. Then I wanted to open a drawer, but once again, the snakes were in the ground just beneath the drawer. I came upon snakes again in the earth at the opening of the outside doorway. As I began to enter, one rose up from the ground. I was alarmed at first, but then I decided to remain calm and not be fearful. I trusted something within me. The snake began spiraling up to me in a very friendly manner. I began petting the head of the snake as if it were a dog; we were friendly towards one another. Suddenly, I began to fly. I was flying through the tree tops saying to myself, "This must be this yogic flying I have heard about; wow, this is great." I was able to fly at will. I awoke.

What does this dream mean?

Stop. Wait a minute. Lying beneath all of this is the hidden God revealed.

The hidden God revealed? Is there a message for me?

The essence of the nature of God is one of true rapture into the unknown. We seek the nature of God on this earth and it is revealed to us as we succumb to the rapture.

What do the snakes symbolize and that we befriend one another?

In surrendering to that which you think is "beneath you," you in fact surrender to that which is You.

What do I think is "beneath me"?

Your Self and all that has been given It to transform the world.

What has been given me to transform the world?

The Holy Spirit.

I do not think that the Holy Spirit is beneath me.

Apparently you do.

Why do you say this?

You have not asked the Holy Spirit to save you yet.

I never thought of specifically asking the Holy Spirit to save me. Save me from what?

Thinking that salvation is far away. It is near, it is here now. Your thoughts are a hindrance to the work of the Holy Spirit in your life.

I am willing to be saved from these thoughts which are misleading.

Then it will be done.

I bow my "head into my hands" and begin to pray. I ask the Holy Spirit to save me from my thoughts about who I think I am. I pray that I am willing to be saved. As I rest in this place, a vision comes to me in which I immediately see crowds of other people who appear to be "homeless." Then I see myself being pulled up off of the earth by my arm. As I rise up another reaches out their hand and takes hold of my ankle. Then another takes hold of this person's ankle and soon there is a human chain of salvation being drawn up by the Holy Spirit. I realize that as one person becomes willing, many become willing. It is in our willingness that we are joined. We all continue to rise up and the human chain keeps getting longer. Eventually, the Holy Spirit pulls us up onto a platform in the sky and we pull each other up onto this invisible platform. The presence of the Holy Spirit is palpable. Now a woman's face comes to me. Her head is shaven. She takes hold of me and whisks me up further.

The following dialogue ensues:

Mary:	Where are we going?
Angel:	We are going to see God. He wants to talk to you.
Mary:	Talk to me? About what?
Angel:	God relies upon His people to bring the earth back to Him as He created.
Mary:	Why?
Angel:	Not for His sake, but for your own salvation, for complete union with God.
Mary:	The physical earth as created?
Angel:	To bring your mind back to God for your own sake and the sake of others.

Mary: I feel like I am having delusions of grandeur.

We come to a stop at another platform.

God: **You are having delusions all right, but not of grandeur. You are having delusions of inadequacy.**

Mary: I do feel pretty inadequate.

God: **You have no duties to perform in my eyes, Mary, but you have duties to perform for your own sake, to bring you back to Me in your mind.**

Mary: What duties do I need to perform to bring myself back to You in my mind?

God: **You are harboring guilt about who you are, as I created you.**

Mary: What will rid me of this guilt?

God: **Feed the people, cloth your brothers, care for the sick, and let the departed minds know they are joined and resting in My Presence. If only they would pay attention.**

At this point, I began running away from God in fear, heading back to earth, as I just wanted to get home. Then, as I was about halfway, I realized that the fear had been transformed into joy and I was now running back to earth to share the good news; that I spoke to God, God cares, and I can rid myself of guilt by serving others and teaching the departed minds to rest in God. As I serve and teach, I see my Self and everyone for who they truly are as created by God. It is only in our own small minds where we believe that we have failed God and are therefore inadequate. So we turn away from God in fear of being punished and abandoned. Nothing could be further from the truth than believing that we have failed God. God is waiting for us to return home so we can see that we never really left, except in our own minds. Let the truth be revealed through my willingness to see it and share it.

I see God laughing as I run away because God knows. God has seen it before and knows the end of the story.

*   *   *

Disturbing the Peace

Yesterday I was wondering if the ego or evil purposely tries to upset me, purposely presents situations to me when I am resting in Stillness, just to upset me. I was sitting at a stoplight trying to maintain the peace I was feeling, when a series of events potentially disruptive to my peace occurred. First, as I was doing some deep breathing, the car in front of me began letting loose exhaust fumes, but I laughed and maintained my peace. Immediately thereafter, as I resumed my deep breathing, I was happy to see the green light ahead and as I drove through it, fresh tar was being laid and I inhaled that! Alright. Immediately after that, another green light, and a pedestrian crossed right in front of my car. Okay, I thought, who is trying to disturb my peace? Then I remembered the dream of the snakes and how the snakes upset me because I saw them as obstacles along my path, but then I chose to not be afraid, to not get upset and react. In doing so, the snake and I both experienced the love of God, and I was then able to fly at will! So, is the message that, "forgiveness lies in the eyes of the beholder" like you said once before? I am not purposely being taunted by the ego or evil, but I taunt myself with my perceptions.

Mystery revealed.

So, when I sense temptations from without, these are really my perceptions?

Not until you realize the power of your own perceptions, will you realize the illusion of temptation.

Mentor Within, how do I "know God?" I sit here, wondering, how to know God.

Mainly through realizing the purpose of your life. How do you think you come to know God?

By being willing to be led by God.

Herein lays the purpose of life.

*   *   *

Passion

I just realized that the best way for me to practice qigong and movement is to teach it. Teaching has been and continues to be an activity wherein I allow myself to be led by God. I find myself enjoying and letting go into the spontaneity of teaching. I have a lesson plan, but I am willing to abandon it and let Spirit within teach. My students applaud me; all I am doing is being willing to be led by God so others benefit because the Spirit of God touches them too. When I teach, move, and touch, I naturally feel the flow of Divinity moving through me; all is well. When people search for something they are passionate about, I believe they are really searching to experience this Divine flow. This is what makes our passion be our passion.

I am aware that I have my hands and feet in many things. I am doing a lot. I love the variety, however I question whether this diversity is keeping me fragmented and stuck and unable to focus. I get tired, scattered, and unmotivated. I feel like I am not really doing any one thing with focus and awareness. I feel it is time to make some decisions about how I am spending my time. Mentor Within, how should I spend my time?

Passion is the many ways God's Will passes through you. The Spirit moves you to realize the peace of God, herein lays passion. Passion for God is being willing to set aside our heart's feast of desires and lofty plans and devote ourselves in service of God's plan.

Do all of these activities I choose to be involved in play a role in being of service to God's plan? What is God's plan, by the way?

All of the days and nights spent on earth bringing peace and joy to others is God's plan. Activities bring peace and joy only through your "presence."

I had a realization today after my meeting with JoAnn. She encouraged me to let my Self be seen and let go of how it is all going to look, to let go of structuring my spiritual journey to fit into some job, program, or hospital. As I stood alone on the elevator, I realized that all I can do is stop trying to structure the external world, the physical form, and focus on the space within me and my relationship with God. In doing so, the external space will unfold accordingly, if I listen and respond to the will of God moving within.

A part of me feels disheartened after our meeting. It is obvious that there is no money at the hospital for what I want to do; I will have to volunteer, but I cannot afford to volunteer very much. I find myself angry over the priorities of the world. The pharmaceutical companies make millions of dollars a year, in part because our culture values quick fixes and symptom relief, not healing. Why do I feel so disheartened?

If I told you, will you believe me?

I am willing to believe you, try me.

(No answer.)

Okay, I will believe you. I truly deserve an answer.

Because you see obstacles at every turn. Nothing finds its way.

I am restricting my own freedom by trying to fit into an already existing format. I feel like I am a triangle trying to fit myself into a square. I am encouraged to let my Self be seen, but I have a false perception of a world structured in such a way to prohibit me from letting my Self manifest and get paid for it. This is an obstacle in my mind.

Truth matters. Everyone who believes otherwise has forgotten the realness of God. Do not resume your old way.

I just realized, here I am looking for a form outside of myself to experience God, to share God. I am the form, there is no other form that could "share God," as I have been created in the image of God and am not separate from God. It is not about finding a form through which God can be expressed. I am the form through which God is expressed.

*   *   *

Seeing the Christ Within

I still today sit in the mystery of a miracle that happened yesterday at the hospital. Bill, a patient on the Brain Injury unit, who had been diagnosed with alcoholism and schizophrenia, made my day. When I first met Bill, he was agitated and throwing punches, one that nearly landed on my head. Today, he was calm and quite sweet. He wanted to sponge bathe after breakfast, but he did not have any clean clothes to put on his clean body. In fact, he had no clothing. He was wearing hospital scrubs and an old shirt over those. I offered to wash his clothes for him and then went to find him a clean sweater from the donated clothes closet. I brought back three shirts to choose from and he chose the brown sweater with the front zipper. At the end of our hour together, he looked at me and said, "You must be tired" (from the therapy session). I looked at him and said, "You know Bill, I was really tired when I got here this morning, but I do not feel tired at all now. You have made my day." I felt renewed, renewed "spiritually," so that I did not even notice my morning fatigue.

Later that afternoon, I brought Bill his clean clothes. At that moment, he looked at me, our eyes met, and I felt "seen." The Christ within me was seen. He said "thank you" with a sincerity not of the ego, not out of obligation or manners. I felt he was saying "thank you for being you, for letting me see your Self." I was floored. We sat together in silence. He thanked me again. Then I thanked him for helping me to feel the peace of Christ within myself. He said with surprise, "I did that?" So today, I still see his wild, bulging eyes conveying the peace of Christ.

I bought Bill a hair pick for his afro and deodorant and brought it to him the next day. I wondered, as I felt so moved, if I was being called to work with the poor. I have never been so moved by God in all of my days of working with people on this earth.

*   *   *

Self Expression

I am torn between resuming my studies of Japanese Life Medicine, devoting my time to bringing movement and bodywork to the public, or working with the poor. Would I have been given gifts that I must set aside?

There is no such thing as being a burden to others.

What does this have to do with my question?

You must see the connection between your desire to use your gifts and your non-acceptance of these gifts, because you see yourself as a burden to others when you share your gifts. You are embarrassed to share your gifts. It is as if you are interrupting their plans and taking up their time or being offensive in some way. This is an obstacle to using your gifts. It may seem implausible to be thinking in this way; however, you are seeing your Self as an obstacle, hence burden to others, as opposed to a gift to be given away freely.

As I hear you say that, I realize that I sometimes see it as a burden to me to share my gifts. I do not want to be bothered. Yet when I let my Self be seen, I feel free, not burdened. When I focus on "talents," I feel burdened.

It is yourself that sees your Self as a burden. The ego knows that it does not stand a chance against the free will of the Self which is the same as God's. The ego instills a desire to use your gifts, but for all the wrong reasons, hence eventually the gifts become burdensome. This is why so many people who pursue their passion fall beneath the weight of the ego's desires. The Self desires to use one's gifts simply as a means of expressing love and healing in the world.

*　　*　　*

Hesitation

I had this bizarre dream this morning. I was in church, a cathedral, and it was communion time. The people in the front pews went to communion and returned to their pews. Then there were several other pews in front of me, where the people did not go to communion. I was hesitating going to communion because I was wondering what the deal was with these people who were not going. Then I was called upon to do healing up at the altar. I began working on a blond-haired young girl by sliding my fingers over the back of her left forearm. At some point, I opened her arm and looked inside to find that she was made of metal like a robot. The inside of the body was just a bunch of parts like a machine. What is the meaning of this dream?

To worship one's self while simultaneously seeking communion with God, makes Spirit indiscernible. As you wait upon others to respond to God and hesitate in your response, you lose sight of your purpose of providing healing. Your focus on the healing of the girl's body, displays that the body is "made up," and therefore cannot be healed. You have avoided your purpose by focusing on body parts that are not even real. In the dream, you were called upon to come to the front of the church for someone needing healing. When you looked inside the person, you saw false ideas about God. This is what you have been called upon to do; discover the false ideas about God, and through your very nature, healing is done.

We can begin again at any moment,
we just need to recognize the
healing presence of God within.

Chapter Four: August

Do not fall prey to your own mind.

Illusions Battle Illusions

I had another miracle with Bill, the patient. As I walked towards the dining room, he saw me coming and stood up to greet me saying, "I saw you coming, so I stood up, Mary." He had made a point earlier that morning, to ask my name and commit it to memory. He was being discharged and I wished him well. He replied, "I wasn't like this in the beginning." I told him that we can begin again at any moment, we just need to recognize the healing presence of God within us. "Yeah," he said. Then he shared that people had been telling him to watch out for Satan and his trickery, in that he may think he is choosing God, but Satan will sneak in and take on the look of God; he always needed to be on guard against Satan. I could see this was causing further conflict in his mind. I assured him that all he needed to do was focus on the healing presence of Christ within and all would be taken care of. He then mentioned that this reminded him of the 12-Step program and paused. As he held up both of his hands, he said, "Yeah, if there is God and Satan (meaning if they are both real), that's destruction," as he crashed his hands together. How profound I thought. He saw the battle between truth and falsehood and the perpetual conflict it perpetuates in our minds as people get caught up in thinking Satan is "real" like God, and pit God and Satan against one another. Or, as we believe our egos to be "real" like God and take them into battle with God. God has no interest in battling and God knows our egos are not real, therefore there is nothing to battle. God knows that what is false is not the truth. I assured him to focus on God. He apologized for his eyes tearing up as he placed his hands over his chest and upper belly. He said, "I am feeling the Christ within ... I am happy I met you." What an experience.

*　　*　　*

Authentic Life

What does your Mind speak to us today?

How often do you maneuver through this day and allow your Self to be seen? It really does matter to the freedom that you seek and crave.

Mentor Within, I am not quite sure what the rest of this book is to be about. Now that I have learned the lesson, "let your Self be seen," what else is there?

Do not forget that you cannot be healed simply by learning the lesson. Powerful wheels have been put in place to alter the course of your life, now that the change is being made from darkness that promotes darkness, to relinquishing your soul to God. The "truth" of the world will no longer dominate.

What do you mean that I cannot be healed simply by learning the lesson?

Be the lessons you have learned.

I still cannot make up my mind about whether to continue with the Authentic Movement group this fall. What do you think?

Not only can you not rejoice in following others, but the Holy Spirit allows movement in only one direction.

This is what I am feeling lately, for the past two to three years. That I am following others in too many different directions.

We cannot hear two voices clearly, God and another. What speaks to your heart always flows in to you and flows outward, becoming Self within.

Authentic Movement is about listening and letting yourself "be moved" by a deeper voice, impulse, the unconscious. What do you think of this?

We cannot judge all of these various practices without also judging ourselves as we choose to participate, to follow or not to follow. Judge not Authentic Movement, but look at your motivation for participation. Why do you think you should enroll in Authentic Movement?

It is a group of women on a conscious journey and I appreciate their seeking.

Who or what are they seeking?

Their authentic Self.

Remind me again, who you are.

The Christ to be seen in the world, through my Self, so that others may also be seen. I realize now that walking the path of my Self through this world, is my authentic movement. Thank you, Caroline (my Authentic Movement teacher), for seeing my Self.

(Sitting in silence.)

*   *   *

Confusion

As I was walking up the stairway this morning, a light went on in my head. I heard an inner Voice speaking to me about something that I was going to do at the moment. I realized that this Voice that I have been hearing all of my life, was not another voice of the ego presenting me with yet another potential choice in the world, a view to be weighed. Rather, this is the Voice of the Mentor Within speaking direct and clear, either telling me exactly what to do or asking me, "Why are you doing ...?"

So often I have battled with this Voice and actually have confused myself by ignoring the Voice and devising my own plan. When I do this, the tension within remains and I never seem to come to a resolution. As long as I cling to my choice, I remain confused. I vacillate and situations remain unresolved. If I was totally steeped in my ego, I imagine that I would not even hear the Voice of the Mentor Within, because I would have made up my mind of how life is going to be and that is that! Like being on a runaway train, there is no stopping or even rest breaks to reflect. Thankfully, I have always heard this Voice that "knows." Unfortunately, I have often chosen not to follow. Confusion comes from my unwillingness to listen to the truth and follow.

*   *   *

Lonely Paths

Mentor Within, I am aware that I like to spend a lot of time alone. This longing for solitude and my easiness within it, however, concerns me. It means that I do not see friends very often and I am concerned that this is not normal or good for a person. I have a lot of contact with people at work, so I am not up for much more beyond that.

Aloneness and solitude are two very different things. One can be alone and never experience solitude because of the prison of one's mind and how we hold ourselves prisoners of the physical environment, such as radio, television, telephone, internet.

I just seem to find the peace that I experience when I am in solitude so rich. Am I fooling myself and being a loner?

Other places and times to be in the world always present us with opportunities to be seen or to hide.

Maybe I feel so alone when I am with friends because I am not letting my Self be seen, nor am I seeing the Christ within them.

Lonely are the paths that we dare to walk of our own efforts. You have done others a great disservice by depriving them of your Christ Self.

What about the time I enjoy being in solitude? Is it too much?

Famous people find it hard to obtain solitude. They are thirsty, surrounded by others who adore and sometimes worship them, and their thirst is never quenched. They remain thirsty. Everyone remains thirsty. No one who seeks the water that heals will remain thirsty.

What do famous people have to do with my desire for solitude?

Famous people also desire solitude.

What is your point?

Every person chooses a path. Your path is not your master.

So, though I choose solitude, others choose community, and still others choose popularity, none of these paths are the Master. We can mistake them for our Master, right?

Seek your path and you may well find your path, but you will still be looking for your Master.

So, I can give all of this concern about too much time spent in solitude and not enough time spent with others, over to God, and listen.

Yes, and you will know the Voice of God by the look on your face. You will seek the face of another when you part ways with the truth. You will seek the face of God within you, when you remember why you came into this world and why you no longer need to pretend the truth is too great for your "little" life.

Why will I seek the face of another when I part ways with the truth?

Because it is painful to look upon your own face.

*   *   *

Blasphemy

I want to spend time with my parents, but it is never enough time for my mother. How can I handle this? I feel guilty and angry with my mother, though I love my parents dearly and want to spend time with them.

Love seeks no boundaries nor differentiates between you and your parents. You were all created of the same love and have nothing but love to share. Worry not yourself about the amount of time spent with your parents. You belong to God. Time is of the essence only when you bind yourself to matters of the world. Your parents belong to God; their lives are not yours to manage.

You crave to please your mother only to displease her over and over again no matter how much time you spend with her. Her openness to your Christ Self is limited because she sees herself as limited, limited by God. This great disaster is born anew each

generation and perpetuates itself in our ugliness that we fear as we look among ourselves for answers to life questions. Generations see themselves as limited by God. Blasphemy this is, that is the irony. Those who seek not to offend God,* turn away from God consistently because in their smallness they judge God as limited in their lives. Herein lies your frustration in your mother. She looks to a God who she hopes will save her while simultaneously believing that God must hate her; she believes God hates her because she feels limited and trapped by a God who has forsaken her by not fulfilling her worldly desires which she believes would bring her real happiness. What a gift God has chosen for her in you. And, how obvious is God's love for her.

So, where do I come in? How do I practically handle this ongoing frustration?

Remember that every time you see your mother that she has forgotten who she is, and this will be a reminder to you that you also have forgotten who you are. Time with her is time to remember who you really are and let your Self be seen, an opportunity to study and witness God in action.

But I cannot do four hours of this. Please, it is exhausting!

The time frame is not important. Gather and listen for what to do next.

Thank you.

*   *   *

Jesus' Gift

Dear God, thank you for giving me life. Thank you for the Christ within. What a gift you have given for me to behold and surrender, to love and to receive, to give and to live. Thank you, Jesus, for showing me the way. Did you suffer on the cross?

(Jesus replies) I do not know how to suffer in the midst of my Father's love.

* See footnote, page 221*

Thank you, Holy Spirit, for being my Teacher. Thank you, Mother Mary, for listening to me. Mentor Within, did Jesus suffer on the cross?

Jesus overcame his physical suffering through the baptism of the Holy Spirit, who cleansed his soul and forgave his image of himself as a crucified body. Those who identified with Jesus as flesh became instantly caught up in the wounds of the flesh; this is because they were immersed in their own wounds of this physical existence and unable to see beyond the body into Spirit. Those who recognized him as the Christ, were baptized with him at the moment of his death, for here too they allowed themselves to be seen. This was Jesus' final gift; he saw the Christ within. And those who became clear, also saw the Christ within themselves.

*   *   *

Prey

How do I stay in touch with my women friends?

As a friend in Christ, you mostly desire also for their friendship in Christ. Imagine their faces and let yourself see the Christ within. It will be clear as to how to be their friend.

Mentor Within, I have been going all day and now here I sit. I meditated and danced this morning. I feel quiet. I feel peaceful. I do not feel drawn to "do" any particular thing. I do not feel overwhelmed with things to do, though there is plenty I could be doing. I am just noticing the moment. I guess I am in the present. I am not obsessing about the past or future. This feeling has never lasted such a long time, an hour and a half! I called two friends. I am cooking dinner. I think I am experiencing the peace of Christ within.

I am amazed as I see the Christ within the people walking by me. Such beauty radiating from a place that can only be God. It is indescribable. How differently I experience my own life, when I see the Christ in others. Thank you, Jesus, for showing me the way. I cannot imagine anything more beautiful.

I had a dream this morning that I was walking around the hospital with a nun and we came upon a place on the first floor; a quiet, dimly lit, and carpeted room that seemed perfect for my work. She told me that she used to do massage in that room, but stopped. She also said that they would not allow me to use the room. Anyway, it just made me wonder about what is really possible at that hospital as far as doing the work that really heals. Sometimes I think my mission is more than this hospital.

It is. Just imagine yourself working for God and your mission will be accepted. No longer participate in the categorization of the world. We place ourselves in categories and seem to appear organized and community oriented; this is what organizations do, and people. "Seeming to appear" is noticeable in the eyes of God and fulfills the "participation requirement" set for us by societal expectations.

So, do not fall prey to the world?

Do not fall prey to your own mind.

*   *   *

Silence

Continuing to feel the meaningless of the external world, I decided to meditate and ask for help. I asked, "Am I to be in the world, but not of the world as Jesus said? Is life a meditative state, contemplation, prayer? If I am to manifest something in the world, manifest Christ, then what is it to be? What exactly is my calling?" I heard while in deep meditation, "My calling comes to me from what is named Jesus." I then began to meditate on Jesus. What does this mean?

Jesus "became" this world. Freedom surrounded him. He walked in ways that prisoners saw Light. He stepped aside from himself and followed the Created which lied before him.

What do you mean, "Jesus became this world?"

He was in a man-made world, however, he trod the soil lightly, moving his feet ever so slightly, so as not to disturb God's plan and make a path his own. He "took on" the world by becoming "Self" in the world.

Do I have a specific material project to accomplish in this world?

You have a specific nonmaterial project to accomplish in this world.

But I want to start an organization, volunteer, help people in a material way. I feel so lost not being productive in the material world. Do I have a specific mission or calling? What is this specific nonmaterial project I have to accomplish?

Receiving the word of God. Relating Christ to others through your own experience. Meditating on the Christ within. Others will know Him through you. Words are of the essence, for words convey meaning. Therefore, spoken words which "talk" (for the sake of talking) are meant to confuse and must be released to the One who knows better. Silence is the immaterial way to God.

Do I call others to join in meditating?

Meditation is a gift that we must each receive when we are ready.

Am I ready to call upon others to meditate?

You are ready to meditate. The power of Silence within is beyond the teacher of a thousand words.

*   *   *

Who is Doing the Talking?

Mentor Within, I am having a hard time letting my Self be seen. I keep getting in the way with my behavioral habits and personality traits. Help! I am saying "yes" when I really want to say "no." I want to be a helpful person. I want approval. I notice that I feel I have to make myself small so that others will feel better, smarter, in control.

Sometimes I act like I do not know something as someone talks about something I do know. It does not make any difference if the person is "lower" or "higher" on the totem pole in terms of job status, education, money, social status, or male or female. It is like I shut down so other people can be who they want to be and say what they want to say. Why do I feel a need to make my Self small?

You have made an image of your Self that makes it seem difficult to attain. In resisting the exposure of your Self, you feel vulnerable in the world.

How can I stop saying "yes" and agreeing to things that I want to say "no" to and/or disagree with?

Surrender your response to God's Will.

But it is such a habit. I respond before I even get a chance to surrender.

Surrender this to Grace and it will surely shine upon you.

Here I am. I do need Grace to give me that pause in which I may surrender my response to God's Will.

When I talk with you and we have our conversations, I feel so clear about who I am and I respond from that place. My energy, words, and movement flow freely. I want so much to be who I am no matter where I am, no matter who I am with.

There you fly. You just said, no matter "who I am with." It will help you to remember that you speak to others out there who are also "I Am." It is not her or him that you are speaking to, for everyone is "I Am" and conversations flow between you as "I Am" and others as "I Am." "I Am" has the conversation.

So instead of making my Self small so another's self feels big, I speak from my Self to another's Self. I see the Christ within another and speak to the Christ within.

You have made a great discovery.

*   *   *

Forgiving is Giving

I worked this weekend and was curious as to how the weekends were here at the hospital. I get tired of trying to convince patients to participate in therapy. So many hate it. They prefer to go to physical therapy and walk. Weekends could be a time for more holistic therapy, addressing healing at a different level. I realize that physical and cognitive tasks are helpful in supporting functional independence. Many people have received a lot of help. But have we abandoned ministry to one's spirit?

I am ready to begin Project Healing and I am not concerned about money. What do you think?

I am responding. We are all in this together. We cannot heal ourselves alone. This is the beauty of Self love; it extends outward to others. Set your sight on God and all will be seen clearly. Do not rely on the eyes in your head for sight; only Christ within has clear vision.

I feel so sorry for this woman I met who is struggling with alcohol abuse. It is so sad to see the destruction when the truth is only a breath away. How can I help?

Forgive her self-image that she perpetuates out of fear. Only in giving can we receive.

What must I give?

Give everything that matters to you over to God; not only the "large" life situations, but the "little" endeavors that annoy you. People's ways cannot harm you, you cannot even really harm yourself, but aggravation can cease the moment you surrender.

*   *   *

Divine Nature

There is just not enough time in the day to do all I would like. It is so disturbing. I would like more time to meditate and pray, but the world calls.

I understand your humanness and your desire to face the truth. It is all within your sense of purpose to want to benefit from divine nature, to relish your time here on earth, and to keep your eyes on God.

I know I can rest with God amidst my daily activities. But I crave silent, still, gentle time with God, a lot of time. I long for solitude.

Most of the time today that you spent with God was quite fruitful. Communion with divinity is a profound liking for you. Convincing you to focus on God even more is taking time.

What do you mean, "taking time?"

No matter what your desires and intentions, time is of the essence, and how you divide it up into its many compartments for futile activities counteracts even your good desires and so-called intentions. Divine nature is not clocked and cannot be compartmentalized like human nature. God is not a blender. God does not take all of our desires and intentions and blend them nicely into a frozen beverage to quench our thirst. We cannot arrange our schedules and days and then ask God to intervene. God will not intervene on our plans. We may eventually self-destruct or become wealthy in the eyes of the world, and then blame or thank God, but God has nothing to do with our planned lives. God has a plan.

You no longer want to live according to the rules of this world and yet you are considering purchasing yet another appointment book to try to gain better control over your life. And it looks good, doesn't it? These nice black scheduling books so neat, organized, and personalized. If only that were your answer.

This is my prayer, "Dear God, show me how to love." It is not about being right, I want to love.

*   *   *

Sacrifice

Mentor Within, how do I begin with *Healing Waters: Project Healing?*

Release. Surrender. Join. Pursue that which joins you to your brother. At the same time you begin, I too begin.

Is it not possible for you to be a little more concrete with me?

I can help you only insofar as you will help.

How can I help?

Relinquish your image of God into the world.

What does this mean?

Teach. Be a witness to Self and the images of the world will be replaced with glimpses of the truth. What appears as sacrifice and strife, will be welcomed by those who have captured the wild self, harnessed its terror, and attempted to train its vain imaginings. For having wrestled with the ego and been drawn into its provocative schemes over and over again, one sees no way out and the end feels near. Sacrificing one's self is no longer experienced as sacrifice, but welcomed as relief from the perpetual unknown chaos of the world.

*   *   *

Awareness is Action

Project Healing is the first project of *Healing Waters* dedicated to what?

Healing Waters cannot respond to a need that people do not even know they have. When one is bleeding, but does not know, one will not seek medical attention. Therefore, the world needs response at the level of awareness, to bring their search for God into their awareness, and to bring their hearts to God. To respond to any "need" in the world that people may think they have, without helping them to recognize their one and only need, will be

a waste of your efforts and a frustration to your call. You begin your steps forward at this level; remember the bottom of the stairway? Awareness of our need for God is the first step.

So, how would you write *Healing Waters* mission statement?

***Healing Waters* is a ministry of love dedicated to bringing people to God.**

Yes. I could have never been that clear and succinct. Now, what is *Project Healing*?

***Project Healing* is an in-the-moment expression of God that pervades the universe, as one allows the inner Light of God to radiate onto others. It is a mission that begins in the heart of every willing human being. One will only be able to accomplish this task through daily devotion to God. The Creative Spirit of God will direct our path.**

I just imagined that at work I could ask therapists to participate in five minutes of centering meditation. Then I imagine people being resistant to this idea because spirituality is personal.

Making spirituality "personal," which is what religion does, is what keeps us divided, separated, and distant from the truth. Those that resist such an opportunity to come together, can look on their resistance and learn from it. No amount of resistance, even the slightest, is worth not being aware of and surrendering to God.

*   *   *

I feel like a "jack of all trades and master of none."

You are God's master plan simply by being who you are. Nobody can be you except you. Accept God's Will for you not to be a professional career person in the world. Your life is a call to God, a commitment to love and truth and bringing others to God.

I feel very unsuccessful in the eyes of God too.

You have found all of the pieces and seen the One.

And what do I have to show in the world, to the world, for seeing the "One"?

You have been given "Life," Life in the biggest sense of the word, which is beyond the life of this world.

But what good is it if I do not bring this "Life" into the world?

You can bring your Self to the world. Only God can give "Life."

So, we are back to letting my Self be seen.

*   *   *

Detachment

I had an awareness tonight about "detachment." At 7:30 this morning, I had a patient who was quite cantankerous. Now, I am not a morning person and I immediately saw where this could lead. However, I noticed that instead of me trying to "detach" from this woman's personality and see God in her through all of that spite she was carrying around, I just chose to let my Self be seen. Immediately, the situation shifted. I felt so peaceful and was able to provide therapy in a loving manner and she eventually started saying "thank you" instead of continuing to literally hit me.

So my sense of "detachment" is that it is a lot easier for me to let my Self be seen than try to practice compassionate detachment. In fact, "compassionate detachment" sounds like an oxymoron, trying to join and separate at the same time. Letting my Self be seen involves only joining, no separation. Mentor Within, what is your view of "detachment"?

Detachment cannot be given freely from an imprisoned mind. All we need detach from is our "own ability." To "detach" implies that we are "in relationship" to something or someone, which we no longer want to be in relationship to, or at least, not in the way we are in relationship to something or someone. We cannot detach from something or someone that we in fact are not really in relationship to in the first place. Relationship implies at least

"two." In real relationship, there is only one. So, once the mind is free, there is nothing to detach from, for a free mind is always joined.

I cannot thank you enough for this answer.

*   *   *

Last night, I saw a movie and a lot of sadness about all of the pain in the world rose up within me. In this movie, "Mrs. Doubtfire," the father really loved his children. Not in a possessive, sick psychological way, but real love, or so it seemed. But because his love for his children did not look the way the world thought it should look, and because he did not currently hold a job that was professional or substantial enough, and because he showed his love for his children in an unusual, carefree, creative way, he was deemed in need of psychological evaluation and was given only court-appointed visits with his children.

I felt sad because I realized that no matter how much real love God poured into this world (I imagine bucket after bucket of water pouring from the sky), it will never be enough because: 1) people do not recognize real love when they see it; 2) we are afraid to receive God's love into our planned lives; and 3) God's love may show Its Self to us in ways that do not fit our expectations or preconceived notions, so we toss it aside without consideration.

I found this all to be very sad and cried quite a bit over the level of pain, sadness, and anger in the world. How can I be of any help if even real love, is rejected?

(I forgot to listen for the answer.)

John reminded me that real love does have an effect even if we cannot see it in the moment. He reminded me, "Look at Jesus."

Though I do not really study *A Course in Miracles* or do the lessons, and in fact I have had many grievances with *A Course in Miracles*, I decided to go meditate. After meditating, I just opened up *A Course in Miracles* and the lesson was, "I will accept my part in God's plan for salvation." I realized that if I do this, God will do the rest.

I struggle with two things: 1) wanting to play a bigger and better role as God's servant, and 2) once I hear the Voice of Light, turning away from it instead of following the guidance I crave so deeply.

*   *   *

Not God

What did you mean by Healing Waters being a ministry of love dedicated to "bringing people to God"?

Many purposes are served when you bring people to God. This is the purpose of your life; between night and day you will make your Self known. You shall cast your shadow onto the world and see it for what it is, something of the world. We become fear for the sake of maintaining our "purposeful" lives.

What do you mean, "Cast my shadow onto the world"?

Let it be of the world for that is what it is. Darkness is not revealed in darkness, therefore it is not seen for what it really is. The more you study yourself and the world, the more you will learn about darkness. There is no limit as to the depths of darkness into which the ego will take you.

The darker my world gets, the more likely I will long for truth and to be saved from my false self.

This is really the only advantage of having a false self: it actually leads us to God if we recognize it as "not God."

*   *   *

Real Love

I forgot earlier to listen for the answer to this question. How can I be of any help, if even God's love, the real love, is rejected?

Real love is never rejected. It is always received because it is not dependent upon the ego to accept it. Have you not noticed,

that when the fullness of love flows through you, there is always a subtle effect? No behavioral changes may be imparted by the receiver, yet at the level of being, all is received. It is always recognized by the Self, but may not be shown at the human level. The ego cannot block the fullness of Love. We have all accepted God's love; we just do not always recognize it at the time. We are the love of God. We seek in circles for that which we can only find inside. You can be of help by seeing the realness of the Light and entering into it.

I am aware of subtle changes in people as real love flows. It is recognized on another level of consciousness. Like a "spiritual smile" that the face cannot mask.

Nothing can mask the realness of God.

As real love flows through me and out into the world, will it have an effect on the world?

The "effect" is you. You are the effect of real love. Real love recognizes Its Self in others.

What good does recognition do?

It removes you from that to which you believe you belong, the life of the world. You belong to Love.

I had a dream last night. Ruth, a friend of mine, was dressed in soft textured silk of orange, red, and gold. As she lounged on the window seat and I melted into her softness, she spoke sensuously, "My longing is the longing of the tallest trees." It was a moment of shared love and longing ... for God.

By being love, can I reduce poverty, hunger, spiritual deprivation, abuse?

By being love, you recognize the self-hatred, and you love anyway.

Then what becomes of self-hatred?

Self-hatred eventually dissipates.

So, the goal of love is not to reduce the self-perpetuating ugliness of the human condition for its own sake, but to let love be known, to be seen. Herein lies the only healing that need be; all else will simply fall away.

The purpose of love is to let Its Self be seen.

I am ready for happiness. Much of my life has been searching for happiness. The right job, the right relationship, the right situation. I am ready to be happy now. I am ready to go ahead and live life. Time passes whether I live it or not. No amount of what the world has to offer can continue to make me unhappy. I will allow myself to be drawn more deeply into Stillness for here is where all happiness is found. I will do only that which brings me happiness, so that I may bring happiness to others. Ironically, bringing happiness to others is what brings happiness to me. Wow. Herein lies my purpose in life: bringing happiness, bringing joy, to others. What a clear, precise understanding of my purpose. I bring happiness to others by letting my Self be seen.

What a way to spend a life: bringing happiness to others, which is found in God.

I often find myself getting caught up in all the different things that will make different people happy. This gets tricky because I would have to be like Santa Claus giving everyone something off of their wish list. Whereas, bringing my Self to others, brings God, brings Happiness.

*   *   *

One in the Same

I am feeling absolutely beside my Self today.

I had prayed and meditated this morning. As I saw so many paths lying before me and found myself getting wound up tighter and tighter, I said, "Please Holy Spirit, direct my path." Then about one hour later, I heard the Voice telling me that my purpose on this earth is my spiritual journey, to unfold before God. My main efforts and energy are to be put towards my spiritual path.

I just had an "aha" moment. I have been approaching and perceiving my spiritual journey and healing practice as two separate things. As if the healing practice is "in the world" and my spiritual journey is "not of this world." I feel a constant countertension between the two like they are opposing forces. I just realized that in resisting the healing practice, I am also resisting spiritual movement. The key is not to get lost in the body and cling to the body as the way. Relinquishing my mind to God is "the way." It is more like an "out of body" experience. In and of itself, the body is only a mode of transportation and communication while I am connecting to Spirit.

Now I feel free to pursue my healing practice because I see it as a way to God, as I relinquish my mind with every touch, every move. The healing practice is not separate from my spiritual path; they are one in the same. This is the truth rising up inside of me, being birthed like the insects in my dream last night.

I dreamed that I had been bitten in three places on my ankle. As I examined the spots, I could see that the insects that had bitten me were implanted under the skin of my ankle. A friend suggested I pull them out by their wings, which were protruding. As I pulled them out with a tweezers, they were literally coming back to life. They expanded immensely and were filling, growing. I was experiencing pain as I witnessed the insects birthing themselves. As they "came back to life" for their "rebirth," they manifested fully formed bodies, then they seemed to die, dropping their physical form, yet the life within had surrendered to something much larger.

I am reminded of Jesus on the cross. A moment before his death, he too was reborn as he surrendered his mind to God and accepted Christ. Then upon his complete acceptance, he dropped his body and joined with the truth.

Mentor Within, what do you make of the dream with the insects emerging from my ankle, dropping their bodies, and surrendering to something beyond their bodies?

Take away the false self and you have nothing to be freed from. Between death and life roams an echo of innocence. We

cannot be kept apart from God no matter how we strive to be seen in the world as the builders of images.

*   *   *

Dismantling Beliefs

I am in a place where I realize the time has come to make some choices about my life; to fully immerse my Self in my healing practice.

There are a few beliefs that must be dismantled before you begin your practice. First, give up your "self" as it appears in the world.

What do you mean?

Ignite the fire of truth in everyone you practice on by not accommodating their personal "needs" for you to speak unceasingly about that which is irrelevant.

What would be considered irrelevant?

You can sense it the moment it rears its head. Stay focused. It is all that is not true. Let your silence be heard.

What is another belief to be dismantled?

What happened to you yesterday is not a predictor of what God wills for your future. This is the second belief to be dismantled: that your past environment determines who you are today.

Okay, what is the next belief to be dismantled?

You cannot make others happy. You can be the bringer of Happiness, but they have a free will to accept or to turn away.

What is the fourth belief to be dismantled?

"Freedom in the world" to live "according to the world," will get you what you want. Nothing is further from the truth. God wills true love for you, and nothing you do, want or desire can change God's Will for you.

I am considering doing another bodywork training coming to St. Louis. How will I know whether to do it?

You will know beneath the surface. The work in and of itself is superficial, but you may bring a deepening to it by letting your Self be seen and sharing it with others.

I have decided to do "Prayer Companions," which is a continuation of *Bridges* in which one prepares to become a spiritual guide. What can I gain from this? What can I offer?

You will gain that which you offer. Nothing need be offered other than the truth. The rest is yet to be accomplished.

Though he is standing in a body,
he knows the body not in the same way.

Chapter
Five: September

Being lost is one of the most
significant paths to God.

Accepting My Mother?

Why is it that I have such a difficult time letting my Self be seen with my mother?

There is a deep union with God that exists for you through acceptance of your mother. Every part of you remembers who she is, but the force of one strand of the "self" in you has the strength of a thousand forces to resist the truth.

Why would I be so resistant to this truth of who she really is?

Because it is who you are also; she and you are one in the same.

How are we one in the same? I know "in God" we are one in the same.

The reason you see your mother as so different from who she really is, is because our real beauty is so magnificent that the darkness of all the forces of your ego could not withstand it, hence your stubborn refusal to see your similarity, your real beauty. Seeing only the differences keeps you bound and gagged in her presence.

That is how I feel in her presence sometimes. I have to bind and gag myself to prevent an angry outburst.

The ego will attempt to bind and gag your true Self every opportunity that beckons its call. You have a history with your mother that surpasses a thousand lifetimes. No matter how many lifetimes you are given, healing will not be received unless you agree to let her true Self be seen by your true Self. Acceptance of the One who brings union.

*   *   *

Peace vs. Emotion

Sometimes when I feel peaceful, I hesitate to enter a specific situation that generally disturbs my peace. I wonder about these times.

Maybe I am not really experiencing peace, but some "feel good" emotion. How could real peace be so easily disturbed?

Relying on God brings real peace and happiness. Disturbance of our peace arises as we grow towards reliance on our self.

Am I experiencing "real peace" or a "feel good" emotion?

Peace and emotions are very distinguishable from each other. One brings peace, the other temporary satisfaction in the world, respectively.

I am aware that when I have experienced peace that it did feel different from satisfaction. The latter depends upon external circumstances, whereas peace is present regardless of external circumstances. Is this the difference?

Recognizing that you belong to God — this is the rising of peace.

Life feels so different when I am at One with Love. I realized today that with my spiritual journey, I have never been able to just accept what I read in a book, what I heard someone say or the values and beliefs with which I was raised. I have had to come to the truth. It is not an understanding of my intellect or a fleeting emotion. It is a "knowing" that thoughts or feelings cannot contain.

It seems as though the truth just rises up within me. It has resurrected Its Self within me. I am the truth resurrected; "I Am" is the truth resurrected. I am a child of God, created in God's image.

I loved giving this massage this morning. I love listening and letting the Creative flow. I am flowing as I let my Self be seen more and more. There is such a sense of freedom when the true Self is expressed.

Mentor Within, what do you want me to do with this book? Are you going to help me organize, edit, promote, and sell? What is your role in getting this book out to others?

You are the walking book. It appears to just be a book with pages, print, and a title. It is you who brings life to the words, the ideas, the passion, the reality.

Is there more to be written?

There is always more to be written. Even when your lips dry up and your tongue is still, there is more to be written.

Do I keep writing or will there be a second book?

Listen to what you have been a witness to. Be ready all of the time.

How do I organize the book? Chronologically, topically?

Order your new life; the book will be organized.

How do I go about ordering my new life?

Practice being You in everyday situations.

I realized tonight as I was in the shower, that I need to spend the rest of my life dedicated to serving others. There is no other option any more. Nothing else calls on me. If I am to grow old in this body and die no matter how I spend my life, then why not spend it serving others. As I have this awareness, I feel the peace of God move through me and certainty rise up within me.

Rest easy, my child. Let your Self be shown the way. Pass on all that matters to others; all of the things of this world. Let the peace of God be your guide; let the Holy Spirit be your ruler. Calm are your nights and blessed are your days. Join me in Spirit — forgive.

*   *   *

The Smaller Ones

Mentor Within, I ran into a former coworker the other day. She invited me to come and observe the pediatric facility where she works and commented about how well I would fit in there. Many people have suggested to me over the years that I work with children because of my movement training and my calm nature. What do you have to say about me pursuing work with children?

For the smaller ones, even greater preparation is needed for they are in many ways, "owners of the truth." They share a closeness to God within their perplexity of this new world they have chosen to enter. Few have come without a very specific agenda to have their personal truth made known in the world. They are in a fierce battle with God to take their position over God. The conflict is quite intense during the first few years of life because of their calm, quiet memory of the peace from which they came, combined with the hunger and thirst for their place in the world. Even the wisest of wise struggle unnecessarily with children; oddly enough, each torn apart between God and the world, though for different reasons. The wise one knows the ill-fate of the world; the younger one remains innocent, sensing all the "possibilities" in the world.

What do you mean by "greater preparation"?

Their egos are full of tricks and can easily fool one who is still under the veil of darkness, meaning that you would play a crucial role in either dispelling the darkness or becoming further immersed in the darkness along with them.

How would one prepare to work with children?

One must be on solid ground, and mostly, easily recognizable as a giver and receiver of only truth. The child's ego will take full advantage of your disguises, fake moods and smiles, and willingness to succumb to his or her self-absorption.

Well, this sounds like quite a challenge.

It remains a challenge for most adults.

Many of the children have some type of disability. Does this make anything different?

Do not allow a "disability" to pull you further into darkness. The Light is available to all.

So what do you think of me working with children?

A mother of a child in the world, you are not. A parent of a child in the world, you are not. However, for anyone to idealize one's work or claim complete knowledge of their field of study, hinders us all. At this time, I cannot imagine you returning to a hospital setting except as a healing practitioner so that the work may be done.

*   *   *

Self Employed

Is there something I could put on my business card?

Give them your name and number. Offer freedom. You are a volunteer. You must decide if your efforts to participate in a business are constipating your mind, therefore obliterating your real purpose.

As soon as I start thinking in terms of a business, I feel torn, confused, and immobilized. Constipated is a good word.

Your ultimate goal is becoming the peace of God.

I remember hearing years ago not to charge for my services. It came so powerfully and clearly. I have never been able to trust this Voice because the world tells me that it is absurd not to charge, that everyone charges. With whom do I begin my services?

Especially be observant of those souls ready to initiate daily contact with God.

How will I know?

They will show a wide open acceptance of your gift of love. Do not judge their belief system.

I imagine a church of silence, where the word of God is spoken through touch, movement, and meditation. I wonder what it takes to start a church; a place to come and listen to God, be a vessel for the Holy Spirit, a vessel for the love of God. A silent community whose mission is ...?

Your mission is to celebrate the joy of Christ moving through you.

I just had a wonderful Trager (movement education/bodywork) session with a wonderful person, Mary. She spoke of a physical therapist she once knew who wanted to be a dance therapist, but she never followed through on her inspiration because she fell prey to other people's expectations of her; expectations based on their fears. She shared that this woman is now living in an ashram. I loved hearing this story. It strengthens in me that if we let God, God wins out every time. God's Will far surpasses the human will, if we succumb to it.

Mentor Within, I am aware that I often feel anxious and sometimes fearful before I am about to give a healing session. Once I begin the session, I feel tremendously thankful to be resting in the healing Presence. After the session, I feel emptied and clear. This cycle repeats itself with every session. What is this about?

What is it that scares you?

I feel afraid as I try to be "a certain way" during the interaction at the beginning of the session. I want to be nice and accommodating and appear "normal." I feel like just cutting through all the façade and saying, "Okay, go ahead and get on the table, find the silence within, and I will be with you in five minutes." I do not want to care if they like it or if they will return for a future appointment. I want to work with people who are serious about healing. I guess this is why volunteer work sits better with me; I do not have to be a certain way to drum up business. The nature of being in business means having to provide "customer service" in a way that looks good to the consumer. For me this pans out as being fake. I hate it and it causes me anxiety.

Then do not do it. Cultivate silence in your mind, only a few words need be spoken to express yourself freely and clearly. We become One when we enter the space together.

How do we "enter the space together?"

By succumbing to the will of God.

What exactly is the anxiety I feel?

A profound sign that you have convinced your self that you are alone In this work. That you are alone, period.

Ah, so this sense of aloneness creates turmoil within me.

Being lost is one of the most significant paths to God. You feel God's absence and this creates anxiety and fear. On some level, you would rather lean on self-reliance. This prevents healing from happening. Healing can frighten one because one cannot imagine what part one would play in a healed mind.

What part do we play in a healed mind?

The part of the giver and the receiver.

How is being lost one of the most significant paths to God?

We choose belief systems that create patterns in our mind and often neglect the reality that exists before us. Being "without God" is being lost. We experience being without God whenever we exchange our Self for that which we think we love, but in fact do not even know what we have exchanged our Self for.

How does this lead us to God?

We have exchanged our life for hatred, jealousy, envy, success. We have endangered our lives and gotten nothing in return. We face death, the inner and outer; we come to know darkness. At last our plates are empty, upon which we feasted, and now all that remains are scraps. Being "without God" leads us to God.

Sometimes I fall prey to being a victim of the world. I hate this fall. I feel useless, powerless, hateful, unforgiving, blind, and angry. How does being a victim keep us apart?

A victim is subject to the will of external forces. You externalize yourself as a victim. You see yourself exposed and vulnerable to a careless, reckless world.

How do I stop victimizing myself?

Be your Self.

I had a dream the night before last that my hair was full of large moth-type insects and another person and I were pulling them out. Then on the top of my head were big, beautiful butterflies. I picked them off one by one and set them free to fly, but they kept coming back to rest on top of my head. Then this morning as I sat outside eating breakfast, a beautiful, golden butterfly came and rested upon my leg for a long time.

Today I am getting closer and closer to coming to believe that my work is not in the physical realm, though I will use the physical as a mode of transportation and communication. There is so much healing that needs to take place, so many waiting. The physical - our bodies, are so fragile, so vulnerable, so fleeting; in and out we go, so change-able. As I grow more and more into Spirit, the less I want to participate in physical activities for the sake of "physical gain." This includes exercise, even Tai Chi. What is going to happen to me? I am going to fall apart. I have no desire to exercise to maintain or strengthen my body. Do I have to care for my body in this way?

Right now you have been given the real gift of addressing other people's spiritual realms through the concrete of the body. Withdraw from your physical (exercise) practices at this time.

What about maintaining my body and my health?

Keep meditating. Emphasize the spiritual in your life.

Cannot some of these physical practices also be "spiritual" and centering?

What really matters (in regard to physical practices/exercise) is that you have a tendency to become invested in the physical realm.

So, when I do yoga, Tai Chi, dance, I am acutely aware of my body, I strive to improve the positions and movement and in doing so I become more invested in the physical. Is that it?

When you insist on focusing on the physical plane, you leave no room for the Spirit to enter.

I decided not to go to Tai Chi class tonight and instead to follow the nudging within to just move, to allow my Self to move me. I felt the unwinding as I gave in to my Self. It was as if I was just following instructions, with no judgment of my body or the moves it made.

What about this method of physical activity?

Use your body to the full extent to which your Self allows you to use it.

This way of moving is a relief from my analytical, judgmental mind.

We cannot change God's plans for us.

I imagine sharing this mode of movement with others. What do you think?

I do not think. I Am. Very simply put, I see people responding according to their various levels of need.

Need for what?

Need to experience their true Self.

What would be included in such a class?

A healed mind — mainly yours, or this will just become another business idea.

Mentor Within, what do you mean by you do not think?

You may notice that real thought remains unshaken by the laws of the physical world.

What does this mean?

My thought is in the undisturbed Mind. Disturbances of the physical world fall easily onto a disturbed mind.

What is a disturbed mind?

A mind thinking on its own without guidance of the Holy Spirit.

When you say, "I do not think," you mean that your thinking is of a Higher Mind.

Yes. But I am available for real thought with you, with everyone.

I am considering seeing clients at my home rather than getting an office space.

Leaving that space within your mind that is overcrowded and

full to the rim, opens the way to new places and spaces that have been emptied and await your presence. Cold, hot, black, blue, these are qualities of environmental spaces. There is nothing worthwhile for you here. Spaces have boundaries and limitations as you have just found out. The physical space is you whose boundaries are love itself.

Where do I see clients?

Outside of your self, your small self.

Where is outside of my small self?

Everywhere you really are.

Where am I?

Most definitely you are that which a space of physical limitations cannot contain. I am everywhere. Office space was not a concern for any great master. Nothing is impossible. We all have our moments, but we are here now for more than mere moments. Life is waiting here and now. Take your business away from spaces and walk towards those who are lost, waiting to be found.

What do you think about my idea for a "Healing Fitness" class?

Be aware. Walk slowly.

We are all called upon to answer our calling from the Holy Spirit; few respond. Most of us are never going to respond in this lifetime. We are too busy. Yet everyone continues to search.

I see now why *A Course in Miracles* states that the ego wants us to "seek and do not find." This is so true. What is the answer?

The movements that we go through in this world are just day-to-day motions, that is it, nothing more — the laws of physics in action keeping everything going. In and of themselves, the movements are meaningless. Our minds have fabricated an entire world by assigning symbols to the body and the environment and the interaction between the two. It is all a figment of our minds playing. We could change our minds at any moment and our world

will change with it. The mystery is in the meaning we assign to the world, because it is constantly changing.

*   *   *

As I begin to clean up and organize my home office space today, I found myself hesitating. I had just purchased and assembled a bookcase. I had been thinking that I probably really need at least two bookcases. Then I paused. I glanced at the stacks of books around me — mostly textbooks — feeling clueless as how to choose which books would go on the shelf and which books would go into storage. As I contemplated, I realized that only a few books seemed important enough to put on the shelf. I went from wanting two bookcases to not being sure why I would need one!

I paused again. I sat down in my office chair, rolling back and forth, my arms and hands up on my head, a moment of contemplation. I laughed as I thought, "Why do I need an office anyway?" As I looked around the small room at my desk, computer, and files, I asked Holy Spirit, "What is the purpose of this office? What is supposed to happen here?" I have an office, now I need a job. I just laughed. Silence.

*   *   *

A Call to Innocence

Mentor Within there is something so remarkable about this two-year-old little girl I met where I study Tai Chi. I saw her staring out the window. When I went inside, she immediately came up to me, stood at my feet, and reached her arms up for me to lift her up. A woman said, "She thinks you are her mother." I squatted down to her level and she leaned into my chest and put her sweet hands gently on my thighs. I asked who she belonged to and her father responded a few feet away. He called her "Laura" and reached out for her as he was ready to leave. She turned her head away from him and held on to me. She was so precious. The following week, a similar episode occurred. What is the connection between this child and me?

God loves you through her; she represents your hopes, longings, and love. She is resilient, precocious, witty, and strong. She resembles you. Perhaps you will meet her again and more will be revealed to you more clearly. Love her as you would any child and the vessels of spiritual truth will immerse you further into your role as teacher and child of God.

I remember a dream I had a few years ago. A baby appeared directly in front of me and said, "You are supposed to be my mother, but if you don't that woman over there will be." There was a single woman with a child in the background. Was I supposed to have had a child? What does this dream mean?

To become one with God all that is necessary is being in relationship with God. Innocence plays a major role in this relationship. The child in your dream calls you to innocence.

Who is the woman with a child in the dream?

A close friend of yours who needs to be called into innocence. Overwhelmed with guilt, she seeks pleasure.

What is she guilty about?

A realization that she cannot sustain herself.

How does this produce guilt?

She cannot bear the thought of dependence on God.

Who is this close friend?

You know her well. She sleeps beside you in your bed at night and whispers thoughts of "sustenance" in your ear, claiming she will sustain you. But a part of you knows the real Source of your nourishment and so you never fully give in to her "logical" persuasion. This is what saves you, Mary.

So, this woman is me? A dark, unknown aspect of myself who betrays me.

She is not the real you, but you perceive her as such, hence she affects your thoughts. She, in fact, is a thought.

The False self-Critical Voice

What do I do with these thoughts that engender fear of dependence on God?

Give them up to God and you will not be forsaken. You have allowed yourself to fall into the trap of self-sufficiency.

I know I have. It is a death trap, a tangled web from which I fear escaping for then I will be thrown into the void. I wonder if this self-sufficiency is where that self-critical voice emerges, the one who tells me, "Look at what time it is, what have you accomplished today?" "You are unsuccessful in the world, you are not a mother, have never had or raised a child, you do not have a successful career, you do not have any money. The only thing you have been successful at is being a student, and maybe your spiritual journey."

I have put a lot of time and energy into my relationship with God. I want to talk to this voice which jabs at me 40 times a day. Who are you? Can we talk? What do you want? I feel the voice retreating as I ask these questions. You are just a bully bluffing, full of hot air. Now I feel you getting stronger, when I insult you, you feel threatened. Who are you and what do you want? Maybe we can be friends. Do not be frightened of me. I can see where my stubbornness comes from.

I now begin a brief conversation with this "self-sufficient" self, the small self:

Mary: What if you just shared one thing about yourself?

Small self: I am never good enough for you.

Mary: What? You are always telling me that I am not good enough. What do you mean?

Small self: I feel insufficient. You never listen to me.

Mary: What is it that you want me to hear?

Small self: I cannot love you the way you want me to love you.

Mary: Why?

Small self: I do not have the capacity for love that you require.

Mary: I am not even asking you to love me. I just want you to stop badgering me. Can you do that?

Small self: If I do that, I will have to be silent. If I am silent, I will have to hear my own thoughts. I do not think I could bear that torture.

Mary: Oh, so you are also being tortured? Some voice is criticizing you. Who is that voice?

Small self: I do not know, but it never stops.

Mary: Have you tried talking to it?

Small self: It does not have the capacity to hear. It has become detached from that part of itself that was able to listen. It is like a tape that just plays.

Mary: Ah, I see. Maybe that is why I am writing this book about listening to the Voice within. Somewhere along the line, I stopped listening. I became detached from that part of me that was able to listen, my Self. Then you became extremely loud and critical of me because you wanted all of the attention. For others it may be a different small voice attempting to drown out the One who knows. Then I let you undermine my faith in listening to the Voice within. Mentor Within, why can't you intervene in this havoc and override the voice of the small self?

It is not that I do not hear the self-critical voice badgering you. I do.

Then why don't you send it love so that it may be transformed?

Once again, I do send love, nothing but, but the self-critical voice chooses not to receive it then accuses Me of not listening.

You listen to me, I am not perfect.

No, you listen to Me. I hear you. I send out an echo that resonates within you.

So, the self-critical voice does not resonate with this echo of love?

You have reached the end of yourself. The self-critical voice is holding tightly on to its self. It does not want to lose you to the truth.

Well, this is a problem because the self-critical voice is an aspect of me that is holding me back.

There is always one.

So, this is my big obstacle. Relishing this voice and hating it at the same time.

One can only hope that you do not relish its survival in place of your own Voice.

How can I stop relishing this voice, hating this voice?

Surrender obstacles.

I pray for the memory to surrender this voice each and every time I hear it, knowing that it does not know the higher Self. Thank you.

What an irony. The self-critical voice tells me that it is not being heard — what a game of the ego. It pulls me into listening to it. The self-critical voice actually chooses not to receive the Voice within, Love. It wants so badly to be heard, that it is not listening to that which can save it from its self.

We each have our role to play in the miracle. Every obstacle we encounter is an aspect of ourselves that is not listening to Love. So, Love, what would you have me do now?

*   *   *

Cellophane Angels

You said that the woman in the dream overwhelmed with guilt seeks pleasure. Why does an individual seek pleasure?

The pleasure one seeks is a false savior. Imagine standing in a window, on the ledge. The crowd below holds out what appears to

be a durable material ready to save you, to break your fall as you jump. You jump. It was a paper towel being spread out to receive you. False salvation is the predator of everyone and you are no exception. Hesitantly, we jump, over and over again, somehow believing that somehow this time will be different. Time is never different. Time is never. We imagine that we have matured and grown with experience, but this is a fool's game, Mary. Let yourself no longer partake of these cellophane angels of the world. Come with Me and see for yourself how true is the truth. The "i" will not forgive you. The lost world will astound even the wisest of fools, but never will you find God among illusions. Give back to others what God has given you. Give back your Self.

*   *   *

Hiding

It really struck me tonight that now is the time to come forward with my real ministry, to stop hiding behind titles, trainings, and techniques. All of a sudden I saw the absurdity of pretending and hiding. I thought of those who have spoken directly of God, spirituality, mysticism. Where would we be if everyone had hidden behind the curtain and not come forward with their real experience? There is strength in being who I Am. Hiding depletes strength and leads to ambiguity, convoluted teaching, and depression.

In the past, I have felt that if I really spoke my truth I might offend someone or scare away potential clients. Well, frankly, I have been hiding for a long time and holding back on marketing my business, because I did not believe in what I was trying to sell; more of the same, more of the physical world. I want to offer a time for people to come together and do movement as a spiritual practice, letting the Self be seen. Not hiding it behind a fitness class.

*   *   *

Lotus Wings

About three months ago, I began to feel a burning sensation in the sole of my right foot. It gradually moved up my body as a tingling, a slight weakening sensation, into my calf, thigh, hip, sacrum, spine, shoulder, neck, and scalp. My right ear feels fuzzy too. Is this "kundalini" energy that I have heard of? What is this pulling sensation?

Okay.

Okay what?

You are blossoming just as the butterfly sitting on your leg yesterday morning showing its Self to you, just as a lotus spreads its wings as petals. Immerse yourself in water, in openness. Resist not the flow of sensations running through your body. All is well.

*   *   *

Our Mistaken Identity

I feel a battle between choosing my ego and my Self; what I think I "should" do versus what I feel drawn to do.

No matter what purpose the body appears to have, it will always function solely as a messenger. However, just as a messenger passes the sealed envelope containing the message from one to another, the body as the messenger is not the "knower" of the message. The Spirit within authors the message and in the primitive world utilizes the body as a communication device. The body is basically a well-oiled machine that wears and tears and takes the bruises for the ego. The ego is like the big bully on the playground that makes its self known particularly to those who fear it. The body defends the ego like a shield in battle, providing protective armor and taking the blows, hence disease and injury. So when we relinquish our body to the Spirit, we surrender the ego which is a false sense of self.

Then what happens to the body?

Cleansing — Purification.

How does one experience a purified body? What does it look like?

The means does not recognize the end.

So the body is the means, but once relinquished to Spirit it is transformed beyond our recognition?

Christ will recover the body and rescue it from its misery. Here signs of mistaken identity are forgiven and we rest in the hands of eternal love, eternal life in God.

*   *   *

The Visit

I had an amazing dream last night, however it did not feel like a dream. Every aspect of it felt so different than any other dream; many of my "spiritual dreams" have more of a visionary than dream-like quality. The dream was more like a "visitation." I got to visit Heaven. I had not died, but I was in Heaven as an onlooker. I watched three people, two women on either side of a man, all dressed in white. It was clear that they had all died and gone to Heaven. They walked merrily arm in arm along a mountainous path. The mountains and surroundings were white with snow, though the path they walked was clear and with no snow. They did not have a care in the world (well, of course not, since they were in Heaven). It was very clear to me as I watched the three walking, talking, and laughing, that even though the environment appeared as if it would be cold, they were not cold. They all wore light-weight white cloth. It was also clear that they had no planned direction or destination. The path was already laid out and they just walked the path. There were no options to consider or decisions and choices to be made. No worry, no sense of past or future. Just Heaven. The essence of this dream was unlike most; the beauty and peace was God sent.

*   *   *

The Holocaust Vision

Mentor Within, I am wanting to change the way I teach shiatsu. The students need to be drawn more inward toward awareness of that which is within. The ego mind is distracting, judgmental, has warped perceptions, and engages in projection. All of these are dangerous for the therapist and client.

The two of you need to contemplate who will be teaching shiatsu. Will it be you or You?

I want more and more for my Self in God to teach.

Well, then I have a plan for You.

Oh, great. What is the plan?

Give up your ideas about teaching. Forget your old practice and methods. Remember, the "mode of transportation" (the body) is quickly "fixed," but seldom healed. Only in unusual circumstances does the body seem to initiate a trigger which leads to a healing of the mind.

What kind of circumstances? Do you regard the body as an instrument of healing?

Why am I all of a sudden having visions of the Holocaust? I am seeing people being brutally handled and forced to live in extreme deprivation. I imagine that at that point the only thing left to do is to turn to God. I am imagining a man whose "humanity" has been broken, taken from him, and there he sits on the hard, dirt ground. He looks around himself and sees the weary, torn lives that look more like death. But in his wisdom, that cannot be taken from him, he sees the only way out is to let God have him. Are these the kind of unusual circumstances to which you refer? This man I envisioned, it seems as though his mind was being surrendered to God as a result of a physical breakdown and destitution. Why am I having this image of the Holocaust?

Suffering often necessitates an opening to God. The vision I have given you is a vision of the ultimate suffering.

But why have you brought me an image of the Holocaust?

The purpose of this vision is to hence clear your mind of all suffering, for this vision holds all of the suffering of humanity. I have imagined you just as you are, and it is here, within you, that I see no suffering. Clearly this is the real vision. I want you to be set free of all the images of suffering that come to you throughout your day and torture your fragile little mind. You have been given the gift of seeing how one's mind can be totally transformed in the midst of suffering by completely surrendering one's weakness to God. Tell me what you see becoming of the man in your vision of suffering?

I imagine a man, no longer immersed in the density of humanity because he has chosen complete surrender. He stands in the dull, cold, lifeless abyss and notices that he has no taste left in his mouth. No saliva secretes into his mouth, for he has lost his "taste" for this world. He stands in the Light that now he sees, basking in All that heals him.

Nothing works as it had before; everything is changed. Though he is standing in a body, he knows the body not in the same way. He has forgotten the body he once inhabited. He is radiant. Everything has changed. In this moment, his is the choice for God. He goes on ... everything has changed ... we have all been changed, whether we know it or not.

You have willingly surrendered your mind to God. The purpose of this vision is to clear your mind for the images and visions that are yet to come if you are willing to receive them, resting in the presence of God. Do not be afraid of the blessings being showered upon you. The gifts of the world are for everyone to receive and relinquish in their own time. The gifts of God are bold and forthcoming. You may receive what you are being given now.

Why would someone be unwilling to surrender one's mind to God?

The mind does not know where it goes most of the time. The unforgiving mind is fearful of willingness, of letting Spirit be the guide, for it sees only the small self which cannot be trusted. Hence, it has every reason to be fearful.

How does one become willing?

When the smallest step is taken toward God, God gives you the walk of a thousand miles that you could not accomplish on your own.

What does any of this have to do with how I teach shiatsu?

Teach. Behold your students in the Light of God. Maintain the Light. The darkness of the ego will negotiate its way behind the door. What you are really teaching is "listening."

How do I rise from the dead,
how do I go the way?

Chapter Six: October

**We cannot know the path
until we take it.**

Mentor Within, I no longer want to put myself in the position of hurting my spine with the work at the hospital. The work is so heavy. What do I do?

Impossible mergers come from surrender.

I surrender the situation to the will of God.

Become the freedom. Set yourself free of preconceived notions of wisdom and purity. What is happening now "becomes" you, in the way of the Lord. Let it be.

Management has changed. Your new employer has a better benefit package that heals the mind with retirement in Heaven.

Mentor Within, I feel scared. I feel fear rising up inside of me. Afraid of the instability of this life, this world, my future. I do not feel safe during this moment.

You feel afraid. You are not alone. Everyone fears their own mortality. When innocence gives way to the "knowledge" of the world, we open doors to many problems. It would be better if you could be among people now and remember your place in the world as a healer among the wounded.

This scares me even more. Having to put my Self out there, to be among the suffering, to participate in reasoning and delusions, to remain a part of the world while living in disbelief of the world's purpose. How can two be one? I ask for consolation. I need to be comforted now.

Be not afraid. Linger awhile in this place.

*　　*　　*

I am reminded of a dream last night in which I was doing body-work on someone for the purpose of healing. I was filled with a surge and flood of Spirit. This uprising moved between the person lying on the table and myself unlike anything I have ever felt. This was a very powerful dream. I felt that it was nothing I said or did that brought on this healing power. It just moved through me. What a gift.

Mentor Within, this sensation around my sacrum is really powerful right now. I am concerned about this tingling sensation running up my body. What do I need to do to take care of all of this?

There where Happiness finds you, I Am standing. There where the precious stones form their beauty, find the miles of earth moving beneath you. Come to where you are and will forever be. Come. Come. Come. And be with you, with Me, and you and Me again. Your will suffers along with its remedies. I know the crescent moon seems only half full to you, and the pain in your foot renders feelings of illness, weakness ... however, sacred prosperity walks together with you.

So does this mean I do not need to go to the chiropractor?

Practice. Practice. Practice.

Practice what?

Healing.

How do I practice healing?

The best way you know how.

And what way is that?

Providing the love that your own heart desires.

*   *   *

Mentor Within, I did a bodywork session yesterday and the person seemed very unable to receive the work. I trust that she was blessed whether she knew it or not, so I guess that is all that matters. I found myself trying to answer all of her questions about the technique and its purpose. She wanted to know the goal. I thought that was silly. She was so caught up in her mind. I just stayed with listening. Afterwards she wanted to keep the verbal exchange on a business kind of level, rather than observing her experience. I went right there with her to the intellect. What a battle this is, to stay with the truth and speak it. I managed to tell her that there was not a "goal." I could have said that the "goal" is to not have a goal, but just be in the here and now. I want all of us to be willing to have our minds healed and to know Divine union. How do I "sell" that without sounding like a quack?

You will sound like something else all right. You will evoke presence of mind in people which otherwise lays dormant. Be the presence you desire to evoke in others.

*   *   *

The Untrained Mind

What a beautiful day. I sit in such beauty. Do you have any advice for me today?

Clear vision arises from within that which is already clear. Rinse your mind of all grief and let yourself be carried on into the healing waters. An open pool of water awaits us.

Ah, that sounds so refreshing. I see myself standing naked in the center of expanding water circles, a pool of new life melting all over my mind. How do I bring others to this healing water?

Quit fantasizing about "reality." Your purity of consciousness saves even the worst of egos. As your mind settles out of rationalizing your behavior, you release others into the hands of God. A lot of requirements await the minds of those still imprisoned. Get out of the way.

What do you mean, "quit fantasizing about reality"?

Reality (the real thing) is seen in the purest of sight and stands side by side with fantasy. One calls us, luring us into deep sleep, frustrating all of our attempts to stay awake. One keeps us awake.

So fantasizing about reality keeps me from reality?

Reality cannot hold fantasy. Fantasy slips like sand through open fingers. There is never enough to fill; the sandbag is always empty. Fantasizing about reality keeps you craving more fantasy.

What do you mean by "a lot of requirements await the minds of those still imprisoned"?

Before rules and regulations there exists freedom. Not freedom from rules and regulations, but freedom in and of itself. Freedom, like truth, stands apart from fantasy, rules, and regulations, for true freedom is seen only in relationship to itself, otherwise it would be seen 100 different ways within relationship to 100 different thoughts, beliefs, or actions.

Imprisoned minds know not of freedom, rather only escape hatches that lead one out of one "framed" thought into another. All of these thoughts framed within relationship to other thoughts quite similar to them, though appearing different to the untrained mind. So one runs from one mode of thinking to another, takes a snapshot, and implants the new picture in one's mind which then serves as the updated version of "reality."

So what are the "requirements?"

Each mind has its own set of requirements that it has chosen for itself. Now of course none of these requirements are real. They are fantasy requirements that keep us engaged in countless searches. Fantasy requirements are like our own individualized computer programs that interface with other programs to keep the fantasy going.

What do we have "requirements" for?

The game states that with each requirement met we are one step closer to freedom. Eventually, we rise to the occasion and see the requirements for what they really are — nothing.

That sounds familiar. Been there, done that! You told me to "get out of the way." What does this mean?

The joy of movement for you is when you do not have to choreograph, right?

When I have a hard time getting out of the way is when people start professing their ideas about whatever and they sound professional, educated, business oriented, spiritual - like they know all of the answers. I jump in there and try to resonate with what they are saying so that they feel heard and so that I sound intelligent. I do not know how to insert what I think and have experienced without coming off abrasive.

Let your Self be. The truth can sound abrasive to the one who believes in that which is not the truth.

*   *   *

Today I gave two bodywork sessions. During the first session, I was able to get completely out of the way and let Holy Spirit go to work. The recipient shared that this was the best bodywork she has ever received. She felt light and as if we were dancing and found herself in the ethereal realm. I found it to be more difficult to get out of the way during the second session. I asked Holy Spirit to take over. Holy Spirit said, "It is not the strokes you do, but letting me be present." At the end of the session I literally felt the presence of Christ lying on the table.

Transferring healing within, that is, attempting to move internal chi from one mode of transportation (body) to another, is where we fall apart and refuse to make room for real healing. Spirit revives the mode of transportation, thwarting all effort; effort is left behind as the person rises off the table at one with their being.

*   *   *

Mentor Within, after meditation this morning I felt that I was losing my mind and holding on to it with a fierce grip at the same time. I kept vacillating between taking the things of this world seriously, like the maintenance man not fixing the light properly and then realizing that this world holds nothing that I want. It simply does not matter that the maintenance man lies about his tasks. I realized that we are all lying all of the time.

I realize that this is a radical message that may hurt some people's feelings or send one into outrage or simply into discounting such absurdity. Yet at the same time one feels drawn to engage and respond on some level as one is drowning in the futility of life and is looking for salvation. It is the feeling I had this morning of being torn between the two worlds.

The healing work I am drawn to is like opening portals into the mind; unwinding the mind, but the body is the instrument. What can I call this work?

Mentoring.

Me, Mentoring?

The Mentor does not have to speak.

I am reminded of this dog I saw yesterday whose owner does healing work and uses the dog in her work. I said to her, "Sometimes it is the ones that do not speak that make the best teachers." She whole-heartedly agreed.

When you say "Mentoring," I imagine you mean helping others to uncover their own Mentor Within by me listening to "my" Mentor Within.

I mean that you do not have to follow the rules and regulations set forth by your culture for healing, bodywork, routine maintenance, love. You listen and others listen too.

This work is like a kind of spiritual revival. Yet language is limiting and conjures up different images, ideas, expectations, questions, and judgments for everyone. No term to describe the work gives it justice.

Presence is Presence — period.

Any way of describing the work can turn some people off. I am thinking of a person I know who feels very defensive about spirituality, which I find odd because at the same time she does not profess to have any sense of spirituality in her life. I know that she struggles with daily existence. Maybe she just is not ready to let God in yet. Timing is different for each of us. What I am really aware of here is my defensiveness brewing as I imagine her response when I share with her what I am doing these days.

These people will not come again.

What do you mean?

Those who choose to find fault with the system (the Voice within) will forego the remedy. Those who receive it, will return either to you, another, or go within for reminders and replenishment. When these receivers of love do return, they return a revealed being; the old self will not come again.

* * *

Temptation

Whatever it takes, Mary, for you to let your Self be seen is whatever it takes. If this all feels unfamiliar to you, that is because it is. It feels uncomfortable to challenge our beliefs about ourselves and others. It is a mistake to withdraw from the world out of fear. That would be fear withdrawing from fear. Nothing can come of this, only more fear — like fear attacking fear. You have nothing to prove to anyone; what is the worst that can happen? Look how healed you are when you let your Self be seen. All that happens is love. You fear love.

I fear who I will become if I let love flow. I love Love in the moment and for the while afterwards that it lasts. I fear losing myself. I fear being outside of myself. In the moment of love I feel total freedom, and to experience this I realize I have to let go of control and sometimes this seems like losing control.

Temptation keeps us finding ourselves binding to self-control. Temptation roots itself in fear. We attempt to free ourselves of superstitions, addictions, hatred, jealousy, envy, depression,

anxiety, obsessive-compulsive disorder, but instead we bind ourselves even deeper to all of these temptations by attempting to fix our personalities as their cause. Our personalities love all of this attention. Gripping our "defects" embeds them further into who we think we are.

What do you mean by temptation?

Temptation is our ego saying, "Come, try this one over here, look more closely at me, behold my fear, relish my beauty, mask this ugliness." The list is endless. Temptation relishes attention.

But are we not denying our faults that are in fact obstacles to experiencing oneness with God if we do not examine them or at least acknowledge them?

The problem with in-depth examination is that when we become the target of our own ego, where does it end? The ego is loaded with faults. Human beings are doomed to get caught up in their aloneness.

I have been through therapy. I have delved, examined, analyzed dreams, introspected, cried, screamed, punched pillows, painted pictures, talked to empty chairs, and kept journals. I imagine it moved me along my spiritual journey. Then again, maybe not. It seems like my basic problems did not really resolve after therapy. However, therapy did support me in taking a closer look at my false self and provided emotional support when I felt beat down.

Recognize your experience. Then let Spirit see it for you. Facing reality will set you free. God will relieve you of all of your pain. You could sit in a garbage can one hour a day and hope for freedom and eventually freedom will come when you really want freedom. There is only one Voice.

*   *   *

Spiritual Teachers

What about spiritual teachers?

Those who have gone the way open doors amidst bolts and fire.

How do I know who has "gone the way"?

They sit behind open doors. Everlasting love in union with God precedes them; they love.

When you say those who have "gone the way," what do you mean?

Those who have risen from the dead. Like a white daisy among a bed of red roses. The seed that has been planted emerges as pure truth.

Why are not the red roses in your description also pure truth?

For they know one another only as a mirror, a reflection of one's small self. They see only that which they believe themselves to be.

What does the white daisy see?

Nothing. It looks within and becomes nothing in its own eyes.

When the white daisy looks within and sees nothing, then what is its motivation to live?

All the red roses, awaiting salvation.

How does the white daisy save the red roses?

By seeing them differently, for who they truly are.

How do I rise from the dead; how do I go the way?

Seamlessly walk in God.

Seamlessly? What is seamlessly?

We cannot know the path until we take it.

*   *   *

The Woman at the Well

Never does it happen that God's vision fails. Jesus saw through the woman at the well.

What did he see?

A woman in love with God, but she did not know it. A woman facing truth, but she did not know it. A woman ready to forgive and be forgiven. This is who we all are. Then one day you see God seeing you.

So this is why God's vision never fails because God sees only that which can really be seen: love and truth. I feel like the woman at the well. Ready to be forgiven. Ready to forgive. Ready to be seen. Ready to see God seeing me. Now, there is a vision.

*   *   *

Hello Thee

I had the most amazing dream this morning. I was asleep in bed and John was in the small dressing room next to the bedroom. He was walking from the windows towards the bathroom. Halfway through the room, he paused and set down *A Course in Miracles* right in mid air with his glasses resting atop the open pages. The book and his glasses just rested right there in mid air as he walked on into the bathroom and closed the door. Then a loud Voice came from the southern window as if directed towards John. The voice was the Voice of God. I have never heard a Voice like this all-knowing vastness. The Voice spoke, "HELLO THEE TO THY WITNESS." I freaked and called out "John, John." Then the book and glasses began flying into the bedroom circling the ceiling over the bed. As it approached me, I reached out to touch it and the book and glasses landed safely on John's nightstand. I felt at peace. Oh, my God. What a trip!

God has left the building!

Chapter Seven: November

**Your routine life becomes
a living prayer of
surrender. Every action
given to God.**

Loss of self

Dear Mentor Within, I feel without cause and effect. I feel no sense of purpose in life. I had no productivity today. How can I come to realize differently?

You have nothing to lose, Mary. Nothing.

I have lost myself. I do not know who I am any more. Who am I?

You are experiencing the loss of the self you made as you entered more deeply into this world. The ties that appear to bind you run deep, but are not tied to anything.

I feel these ties unraveling and each day becomes more meaningless than the day before. Can I stop it from happening?

You can stop the unraveling at any time and immerse yourself more deeply into this world, but it will not benefit you or relieve your stress and strain except momentarily.

Why get up in the morning? Why eat? Why exercise? Why do anything?

Constant suffering is a sure sign that you are fighting with your own will. Give your daily activities over for God's doing. Perhaps you could devise a prayer.

"Dear God, I dedicate this activity to you." How is that?

When you surrender like this to your higher Self, you come to be reminded of your purpose here.

And what is that, what is my purpose?

To surrender your life to God.

Dedicating each activity to God feels less burdensome than me taking on all of the responsibility. I trust that I will be used during that activity for a higher purpose.

Freedom is only a prayer away. Your routine life becomes a living prayer of surrender. Every action given to God. This is the holy life you seek. Remember who you are in real life.

Real life?

The life chosen by God awaiting your surrender.

I want to feel the holiness of this life – not the world, but everyone's life.

Holiness is beyond this world.

Thank you for reminding me of the Holiness within. When I begin to feel like a failure, I will remember my real purpose here - to surrender to the holiness of life. I am planning to go work at a local center for health and healing. What suggestions do you have for me about this decision?

Meet your self around every corner and watch your step. What was once second nature will come apart in your hands. Come by yourself to visit this place where we commune with beauty and know the wetness of the water as it consumes our very being. Growing before us from a steady, calm drip, we have come to expect a full glass of water.

Mentor Within, what are you saying?

Challenge the signs of the times that foresee only death and destruction. Do not succumb to current modes of thinking.

It sounds like you are saying to be aware of fear and joining in agreement with it.

Observe the small self in others and forgive what you see.

What do you mean, "do not succumb to current modes of thinking"?

Resolution will not be accessed by the thought system in which you currently reside, for it foresees only death and destruction as resolution.

How do you see resolution?

Admit that nothing can be clearly seen with its own eyes.

What do you mean by "what was once second nature will fall apart in your hands"?

We cannot underestimate the power of learning. If you rely

on prefabricated means, you rely on nothing.

So what I have learned will not provide the way I do healing work? What I have learned will "fall apart in my hands."

What you have learned will become a nuisance to your new practice upon which you endeavor. The slate needs to be cleared if you are truly committed to a healing practice. Let it reach its own Self out to you. Find time to meditate daily.

Let "it" reach its own Self out to me?

Healing has a Self which extends out to you as the knowledge of your small self takes on less importance in your psychology of healing, which is limited to your own understanding in this place and time.

What is meant by "commune with beauty and know the wetness of the water"?

Feed yourself from the Source and a fountain will be prepared for you which will provide you with the knowledge of your true nature. A full glass of water awaits your thirst.

*　　*　　*

A Prisoner of Love

Mentor Within, I am ready to scream. I just spent three hours with my mother. She really got on my nerves today. Nothing I say or do for her is helpful. Nothing makes her feel good. She has been in total misery since the day I can remember. The way she stares at me and asks me a thousand questions, I feel like I am being stalked by my own mother. Help me!

Fear is the primary emotion experienced by your mother. You have allowed yourself to be drawn into her fearful little world.

Why would I do this? I hate her world. If I lived in her world, I would kill myself.

Does it really matter what her world consists of? Does it really matter? To you your mother represents your ego which desperately seeks you and will reveal its darkest dark to you through your mother just to get your attention.

What do you mean that she represents my ego?

You have carefully placed her on a pedestal to be worshipped and adored and then you crucify her. Both are forms of murder and now you see a prisoner of "love" turned to "hate."

Oh, God, what next?

Remember that she holds no claims on your soul. You may release yourself at any moment.

I think I have tried to release myself in the past by just deciding to love her again – meaning be more patient, listen to her endless moaning, groaning, and judgments, or just stay away when I know I cannot be nice. Sometimes the best way I can love her is to distance myself from her. Why add more to the mess? She rejects all of my attempts to love her. I have felt since I was a child that she wanted me to be her mother, sister, and daughter because her mother and sister were so mean to her. Nothing I did to show love for her was ever good enough. I was never sufficient as a daughter, so how could I also make up for the lack of love from her mother and sister as well?

You really have taken on the sole responsibility for your mother's happiness, only to find the accumulation of everything but happiness.

So now what? My mother feels like a bottomless pit. No matter how much love is given, she is always empty. I give up! I do not know how to love a bottomless pit. I was feeling so good after the session with my client; we were joined in God. Then I immediately spend time with my mother and God is gone – God has left the building! Where are you in all of this?

I am not going with you into your darkness.

I have to pull myself out of this mess?

The ego relishes you in this moment. You are now on the ego's pedestal being worshipped and adored. As the ego observes you in your darkness, it also awaits just the precise moment to take its hatchet and knock you off your pedestal back onto the ground. It lets you take its little place up on the pedestal long enough to replenish your darkness and then tosses you back, this time more deeply into the world of illusion.

*   *   *

Projecting Darkness onto My Mother

So I am asking for your help. I feel this happening. I feel the darkness in me running rampant as I think of my mother. What do I do? I feel terrible, so I know something is not right.

You feel right. Admit it. You feel right in the ways you judge your mother. Of course you have projected your own darkness onto her.

I do not believe this for a second. How am I projecting my darkness onto my mother? She has enough darkness for herself. She does not need mine. Why would I project my darkness? With my client I felt total love just moments before.

The jeopardy of close relationships like you have with your mother is that they provide fertile ground for the projection of darkness.

Why is this?

Nothing could be further from the truth.

What are you talking about?

I heard you say it, but you did not write it down, that the relationship you have with your mother is the closest relationship you have.

(I was thinking that my relationship with my mother is the closest relationship I have and apparently the Mentor Within heard my thought.)

Well, she conceived me in her womb, carried me nine months, gave birth, raised me, cared for me, cried with me, and joined me in happiness. We have been through a lot together.

You have been through a lot together on this earth, but you have been through nothing together until you see your mother truly. She will reveal her Self to you when you are ready to see her.

This is absurd. I am ready now. Go ahead, mom, show me your true Self. I am ready.

Why not look for your Self? I did not say anything about her being ready. I said when you are ready.

I think the only way I can see my mother's Self is by giving her silent healing sessions — no talking; just watching the Light in her rise off the table. I have been putting this off for a long time. She has been asking me for a session for a long time. I guess I am ready.

Thank God!

*   *   *

Looking for the Light

Today I had the most profound awareness of letting truth guide my life. It is difficult to even put into words. As I consider my day, I often get easily flustered trying to prioritize, organize, decide what to do, and commit to or not. Then it all became so crystal clear how the truth is my arrow; it is the fulcrum upon which my world turns if I choose. Then everything just falls into place. I instantly know what to commit to or do next. I know immediately what situation or activity is for me and what is not. It is not that one situation or activity is truth and one is not; it is that I am called to be a vessel of truth no matter where I am.

With truth as my flashlight, my decision-making does not seem so convoluted and relative.

This triggers a memory of a bit of wisdom whispered into my ear a few years ago. I had decided to attend yet another "spiritual" retreat led by a person whom I had hoped could shed some light on my perpetual search for the light. After three days of sitting in silence and just moments before the bell rang calling an end to the retreat, I began telling myself what a total waste of time this had been. The things I could have accomplished in my worldly life in these three precious days. Then in the last moment of silence I heard, "A blind man does not need a flashlight." I laughed to myself. The bell rang. I opened my eyes. Here I was again. Another fruitless search looking for the guru to fill the emptiness and show me the way to the promised land. Here I was again. Blindly looking outside of my Self for my Self. Here I was again. Looking for the light in the darkness. Later, I had to laugh again as I recalled my unsuccessful search for a required flashlight I was to bring because the path was so dark between the meditation center and where I would be sleeping. Funny, on some level, they actually had already told me to bring my own light.

Suddenly the direction for my whole life is clear. Truth does not send me out in many different directions, rather it rests clearly within and shows only one direction — truth. Hence, truth is both the source of Life and Life itself.

Mentor, what do I say to people when they speak such nonsense about life, to help redirect them towards the truth.

I cannot give you a tidy, little profound statement. As you live the truth in your life, the "what to say to others" part will just happen.

Help Wanted Sign

Mentor Within, when the rabbi asked at the talk today, "Who wants to be a saint?" I raised my hand. I hesitated at first, thinking it was a trick question. He repeated the question and finally I raised my hand along with another woman who sat behind me. I do want to serve God and I want to serve the God in others. I see the sign now:

HELP WANTED

Seeking Higher Self to fill creative position.

Must be willing to forgive.

Apply within.

Today.

The truth of this matter is that no one whose purpose in life remains unclear will be able to serve God.

Does my purpose in life remain unclear?

What has its grip on you, Mary, is that you want to grasp your total purpose in life. I want you to recognize the truth within. Practice this.

I am aware of the truth within myself, but you are right. I am not being disciplined enough. I am still falling into my own and other's trappings or that which is not true. So, I guess practicing recognizing the truth within is how I can serve best right now, one step at a time.

It has become so clear to me that my only choice is the choice for the truth. My focus is on listening to the higher Self and following the Voice within as I assist another in opening up their mind to the Voice within. Is this all a figment of my imagination?

I will find it impossible to believe that you have forgotten your Self by believing this to be a figment of your imagination. After having committed such an error over and over again, you could no longer continue to bear witness to the false self. I am not a fool and neither are you.

*   *   *

Return Flight

Can I betray my Self?

We cannot hear One's heart when we bring the ears of the self to bear witness, for the self can only bear witness to false teachings. To believe that you can betray your Self in God is based upon the theory that you can turn away from God. You cannot in reality turn away from Whom you belong. Those that appear to be turning away from God are really turning toward the small self, but God is everywhere. Even when one appears to turn away, though they have lost their attention, they have not really turned away. This is why it is always easy to return to God, because you never really left.

A part of me tells me that I am a fool. A fool to believe that I could really make a difference by following the truth. A fool to believe that I even know the truth.

Physical healing offers only temporary satisfaction. Within the depths of the mind rests a place that knows that one has already been healed and is whole. You dedicate your Self to finding and recognizing this place in others, thereby assisting them in finding and recognizing this place in themselves.

What modalities do I use?

Does it matter?

I am asking you.

I find it apparent that eligible methods available for your use have suffered long enough in the hands of others who abuse them for their own sake.

What do you mean?

Nothing holds water until you completely recognize Realness and then and only then do illusions of thirst give way to the knowledge that thirst holds no reality for you for God has met all of your needs and illusions are seen for what they are, nothing.

How does this relate to what modalities I use?

You have enrolled in a new school of thought now and will gradually be introduced to its premises, which will eventually give you mental clarity.

What is this new school of thought?

I have realized, Mary, that you have been busy playing around with many realms within the illusion, but enough already. We must face the business of reality.

This new school of thought then is based in "reality"?

Do not put me in quotation marks. I Am what I Am. I Am not relative. I Am.

Sorry. I hesitated with the quotation marks. What is a premise of reality?

That there is only one reality.

How will I know reality when I see it?

Too many people and things will attempt to distract you from it.

Was Mother Teresa in touch with reality?

She became one with reality as she served people no matter what their race, religion, color, or ethnic background.

*   *   *

A Holy Glimpse

Lately it came to me to refer to myself by just my first and middle names, "Mary Gerard." What about this?

"Mary Gerard" was the sacred name chosen for you before you were born, chosen by your mother who really has seen God.

So, you have been blessed. We are chosen to heal the world and remind forgotten souls that they are not the remnants of the world, but the holy voices for God. Please work accordingly.

What do you mean that my mother really has seen God?

I have felt her glimpse into Heaven.

*   *   *

Stop Taking Your "self" Seriously

Dear Mentor Within, I have reached a point with my mother where I feel beyond help. I feel that nothing can save me from how I become around my mother. I feel that nothing can save me or this relationship except God. I need a miracle. No matter how willing I think I am to accept her the way she is, apparently I am not. I just realized that I have never prayed that I may just be accepting of my mother. I do not know any more what to do, or what to say, and even if I did know, I know that in my mother's eyes it will not be good enough. Maybe it is true that I am not giving her real love. Is it possible that another human being cannot receive real love when offered? What did Jesus do? I know not everyone received his love?

Everyone did receive his love, but they were still not willing to let go of their world. They were affected even if only for a moment, but their inner resistance remained unhealed because they did not open themselves up to healing.

I feel like I am not opening myself up to real healing in my relationship with my mother because I keep repeating the same behavior patterns that are a sure recipe for disaster. Though today after our time together, I told her that she can forget everything I said because really it has nothing to do with her; it is my problem. What can I do?

Release her into God's hands. Give up your self to God.

I hate that I take other's perceptions as if they are the truth and then try to defend myself against these completely warped perceptions.

How can I stop taking people's opinions and perceptions and making them true?

Stop taking your self so seriously and you will stop taking others seriously. When you are attached to keenly observing your own ego, you may actually reinforce your self. This then also happens with others. You become attached to their egos because if you have to pay the price of being hypervigilant about your ego behaviors, then you want others to pay the price and be hyper-vigilant about their egos. I appreciate your desire to be aware of the ego's tendencies. Be careful however, to not take these ego tendencies so seriously and be so harsh on yourself; you will also be harsh on others. You can instead take the insanity of the ego as a sign to back off.

I guess I want every one to wake up and to stop pretending that they do not know any better. It is miserable for me to live in a world of people faking it, going with the status quo. A person I know justified her loss of faith by saying, "Well, everyone has lost their faith," like that makes it okay. Where does my grim attitude get me?

Right back where you started judging your mother. This can all happen as long as you choose to let it happen.

What will it take for me to choose otherwise? I literally feel like I am in hell and am fighting with the devil; it is that dark.

When you find it necessary to mask yourself to the extreme that you choose to mask yourself around your mother, it can be very disconcerting. You are really not being honest with your mother about who you really are; You are trying to be a good daughter rather than being the loving person you are.

*　　*　　*

Fading Friendships

I love all of my past and current friends dearly, but I have a different understanding of friendship. I do not care if someone does not RSVP, return my phone call or email. I do not care if someone calls me once a week or once every five years to say hello. I have a connection with people on another realm that does not require a lot of specific, made-to-order physical manifestations. It always surprises me when a friend says, "Where have you been, it's been so long since I've heard from you," or "It was good to hear from you because then I know that you are thinking of me." "What are they talking about?" I wonder. I am with them always.

When I bring someone into my mind or they float in unexpectedly, I experience being totally present with one another. There is a joining as I send love and no doubt in my mind that this love is received. I understand that this does not work for many people, especially those who need regular contact on the physical level. I am just tired of struggling to try and fulfill someone else's view of friendship. I am always here for my friends, day or night, good times and bad, yet I am not willing to feed their ego needs.

It floated into my mind that maybe I am not built to have a lot of close personal friends. Maybe my love, time, and energy are supposed to go out to groups of people or individuals in need, within the context of community service. People in these situations seemed to be very receptive of the love I have to offer and I feel blessed in their presence doing God's work. They bring out the best in me.

Dear Mary, you have come apart from "friends" precisely as a rule of one's spiritual life — to become the flower of God for which you are destined.

Are not all destined to become the "flower of God?" Is this not God's Will for us all?

Perhaps you do not fully realize the implications of becoming a flower of God.

What are the implications of becoming a flower of God?

You no longer rely upon the will of others, including the world, to show you the way.

So as I draw away from or watch my friendships changing and some fading, where does that leave me?

Walking in the rain of God.

What is the "rain of God"?

For have we forgotten the loveliness of God's tears that we sit in dryness when the waters of Heaven await our embrace? We have given our selves to the world, reaching for hopes of salvation that will never come. When we come to know God, all questions are answered, for there will be no questions and no answers; there will only be God.

God is not an illusion.

*   *   *

You are the Body of Christ

I arrived at the Carmelite monastery this afternoon for a time of solitude and meditation, only to find the chapel still under construction. A makeshift chapel had been thrown together in a cold, hard, fluorescent-lit classroom. The only saving grace is the altar and a few candles. I am disappointed, as I longed to sit in the dimly candle-lit chapel. I heard a Voice lead me here, why?

(No answer.)

I let my eyes rest awhile upon the blessed sacrament which holds the communion host, "the body of Christ." What is the body of Christ?

You are the body of Christ on this earth. That is the power of the incarnation. Each one of us is the body of Christ. Christ does not have a body; Christ enters the world through you.

Why does Christ need to enter the world?

Christ enters the world with you as your companion.

Why do we need Christ as our companion?

To live fully.

How do I live fully in the world?

Do not take it too seriously.

I take the world rather seriously.

Take your Self seriously. When you question your Self, you question reality. When you question the world including the small self in others, you question that which does not really exist, because Christ is not the world's companion, Christ is the companion of the Self.

*   *   *

Trying to Fit God In

If I am not to take the world too seriously, then what do I do here?

Do not try to heal the world, rather aid in the healing of the brokenness within each person which has been catastrophic — the loss of oneness within, the fragmentation, and the belief in aloneness.

How do I find time to do healings with people, write, and teach? What is my priority?

The wind stirs up the salt of the earth; bellies are full, but hearts are restless.

Yes, so more opportunities arise for healing. How do I find time to do it all?

You have been so busy thinking that I cannot get through.

I know. I am trying to come up with a solution.

The answer to the problem lies in the solution. Your answers

are just that, answers; consequently, real solutions are rarely sought out.

Okay, I hear that, so what is the solution?

Begin your own healing process. The opportunities that present themselves now are not necessarily just for others, but for your healing. It is your work because it is for your healing. Do you have time for your healing?

There are only so many hours in the day.

There are as many hours in the day as there are opportunities for healing.

This writing alone is a full-time job.

We cannot argue.

I simply do not know how to complete all the practicalities of life and make time for healing. You tell me how to practically accomplish all of this.

You cannot have a tidy little functional life here on earth and save souls. The life of a mystic or a saint or one truly seeking God's Will is not orderly, practical, and functional. You say you want God's way, but you keep seeking the world's way and trying to fit God in; it will never work.

No wonder that I am perpetually frustrated. I guess I really have not made God my priority. I have made my "to-do list" my priority and God has become a second-class citizen in my world. This is a lot to surrender, but I can see that I cannot do it little by little because it does not get done at all. I remain in a safe haven infested with the world, feeling perplexed, and, then I wonder why. I fear my life, the organization of my life, going into complete disarray.

You would be surprised how much you perpetuate the disarray.

I imagine asking myself before each activity if I have my priorities straight.

That will be taking yourself into fear several times a day,

because the ego will pull you into the fear of not maintaining functionality in the everyday world. You are not strong enough to resist the fear.

So what do I do?

Stay focused on God. Your mind is God's mind as you give your mind to God. Take God's Will seriously, not your will.

You are right. Thank you.

*   *   *

Pacing the Bridge

Last evening while explaining the darkness of this past week to two friends, I remembered being taken into an image during meditation. I saw vast mountains and valleys with a swinging wooden bridge connecting one area of mountains to another. There I was on the bridge, pacing back and forth between what felt like truth and illusion. I would walk over to truth, pause, walk across the bridge to illusion, pause, walk back over to truth, pause, and meander back to illusion. This is where I am, pacing between truth and the world.

Dear God, I awoke in the middle of the night last night and could not return to sleep, but I still found myself in the midst of a nightmare. I began judging a woman I know. My mind was full of judgments. As I sunk more deeply into petty judgments, I sunk deeper into the darkness. The judgments were torturing me. Then it became worse because I felt myself alone, then old and alone. I had either been abandoned or I had abandoned everyone. In this darkness I realized that in the end, really even now, all we have is our relationship with God. As you know, I turned to you and called on Christ and the Holy Spirit to purify my thoughts, but it was a battle in my mind. Eventually, I wore myself out and fell asleep praying for help.

*   *   *

Dancing with the Illusion

John and I saw a movie about this German conductor in Nazi Germany who, as I saw it, "sold his soul" to Hitler supposedly for the sake of his love of music, his music which he held up to our connection with God, music which nurtured our spiritual nature. Ironic, of course. The character portrayed well the insidious nature of the ego, the things it can talk us into one small movement at a time until we do not know who we are any more. In subtle and not so subtle ways we agree to attack, we go along with violence of all forms, we pretend not to see, we fake it, we choose our small world over God, and we manage to excuse ourselves because we do not know any better or we plead apathy. I am not referring here just to the murder of millions of Jews (the movie was about the Holocaust), but to our everyday interactions from the coffee clerk to our lover to our children. We are a culture of liars.

For myself, I learned how I subtly participate in maintaining and adding to the ways of the world. I do not participate any longer, at least to the extent I once did, as I choose to be conscious of my thoughts and spoken words. This may sound harsh, but when I start dancing with the illusion, it is easy to get caught up in my own choreography.

*   *   *

Holy Spirit, Psychiatrist

Mentor Within, I saw the movie "Awakenings," which I have seen before and I was once again moved and inspired. I was inspired by Robin Williams' character, who saw another way. He was still working within the concepts of what we consider to be a happy life on this earth, which of course varies from person to person. It was not this aspect of the movie that inspired me. The inspiration was the awakening of the Spirit within the patients on the psychiatric ward and within the employees; I would like to play a part in this work.

I recalled what you said months ago about how I will travel to meet with people, let my Self be seen, and allow my Self to be a vessel for God. The movie got me thinking again about all of this. I also recalled past times where I have taught movement workshops to physically and/or mentally ill people, how they responded, and how uplifted I felt to have touched the Spirit within others by using the gifts I have been given and my gratitude for these people who touched the Spirit within me. I remember one day in particular as an occupational therapy student doing a practicum on the psychiatric unit of a veterans hospital. Most of the patients were lifelong members of the ward. One man in particular stands out in my mind. He was tall, lanky and able to move about without assistance, but his movement and interaction with others was minimal. His arms appeared glued to his long, narrow torso as he shut down his gaze to his feet. The therapist shared later that he had been diagnosed with schizophrenia and in the twenty-five years she had known this man, he has never been able to pay attention and stay involved in any task for longer than five minutes. I was overjoyed to hear this because he fully participated in my movement class for an hour and a half. He followed directions and was able to model the simple movements I made, as well as engage with movement props. I was amazed! I saw the Spirit within this man and because of his willingness to open up to that which lies within, I felt the Spirit within me too.

The Spirit moves through you as you allow. The flowers await their gardener.

You spoke earlier of being a "flower of God." What is this?

The ultimate gardener. One who tends God's garden.

What is God's garden? How do I tend it? I am seeing a garden planted in dry dirt with no moisture to nourish the flowers and seeds.

You hold the watering can and quietly pour into the thirsty ground, reminding the flowers of life in the Spirit, which holds no thirst.

I am imagining that I could reach more people by traveling to them and working with groups. I imagine praying, talking, moving, touching, listening, and serving blessed water. What do you imagine?

I imagine a healing ceremony taking place. All come together who long to be healed.

What do you see?

I see people listening to God within.

Providing the inner space for the inner journey. What kind of ceremony?

People come together to bless one another, to recognize their own holiness by seeing it in one another.

This is clearly a spiritual event, not just moving and touching for the sake of moving and touching.

The place for God is everywhere. This is not a therapeutic event though it may benefit in that way. It is a blessed event.

How do we bless one another and recognize our holiness and the holiness of others?

Forgive what you imagine about yourself and others to be true. Even if you imagine that someone is nice, forgive your description of nice because some day that person may pull you off center by acting in such a way that you see as not nice. Hence you will fall into judgment and others will follow suit.

So I must forgive how I have encased that person in my mind and placed him or her in a frame. I must forgive my picture of each person. Then the Holy Spirit will free this person from my judgments.

How can I be the bearer of Light
when I am embedded in the
nails of darkness?

Chapter
Eight: December

God did not go anywhere.

The Nails of Darkness

Dear Mentor Within, spiritually I am feeling very dark today. I realize I am judging myself for not being as "successful" in this world as I feel I should be. This makes me feel "less than" and then I do not have the self worth to go on. Lesson 154 in *A Course in Miracles* speaks of judgment of ourselves as "attempts to hold decision off, and to delay commitment to our function." A bell went off when I read this. I feel like I am holding myself back because I cannot do it all. I am not enough of a workaholic as I once was, so just forget it all! I have no motivation. If God wants me to be of service then why does not God motivate me? I am in deep darkness and turmoil; whom do I choose, God or me and the world?

It is with great sincerity that I address this reply. You have come to face a deep "reality" of life in this world; nevertheless, life in this world continues to perpetuate itself. No matter what choices you make, still others are bound to the ego and their choices are theirs to make. It would do you well to listen to their misfortune and learn from their devious ways so you will not be lured into the pit along with them.

I feel like I am an alien on another planet. Who do these people think they are and what are they doing? Once again, I feel called to devote my life fully to the Lord, to work with the poor in spirit ... to bring Light. But how can I be the bearer of Light when I am embedded in the nails of darkness?

Succumb to the forces that draw you nearer to God.

*   *   *

Take Nothing

During meditation this morning I found myself within an image. A small group of women had come to me, taking me away to prepare me as a bride. I had no clear sense of there being a groom. In fact, the thought of a groom never entered my mind. I told the women that I needed to gather some of my things and take them with me. They assured me that they would be able to supply all that I needed and I did not need to bring anything. I could not imagine that they could supply all the things I had grown accustomed to, yet they assured me that I would be totally satisfied with all of their supplies; my needs would be met.

*   *   *

Seeing the Roses

As I went into my second meditation time today, I asked to come to realize that I will receive my gift once I give my gift away. Then I prayed, to whom shall I give, where should I go, and when. The answer to "when" came immediately, "now." The answer to "who" came next, "everyone." Then I wondered if the gift I had been given was my life. But how do I give my life away so that I may receive Life?

As you share with your brothers and sisters Christ's message of the "Oneness," Life is given.

How do I do this?

Live life as your Self in Christ; you will be giving Christ to others.

How but on occasional instants do I live my life as my Self in Christ? This does not happen often.

Be willing to recognize the Christ in others and you too will be recognized.

I then wondered if I was squandering my life. Am I?

Anyone who squanders their relationship with God is squandering life.

How do we squander our relationship?

Pretending it does not exist. God has a relationship with you even if you pretend that you do not have a relationship with God. Ask for a relationship if that is what you want and it will be given you.

This life I am invested in now is very limited by my body and time, the 24-hour day. So, this gift of life I imagined that I was given was not even referring to this life I have come to know. To hold my individual 24-hours-a-day life up on a pedestal and worship time and all that I am able to achieve in that time, this is not the gift of life to which my meditation referred, is it? Rather, the gift I have been given is eternal life in Christ.

Give. Give. Give. Your life, your real life, is not bound up in your body or in time and space. Your real life is unceasing. It is eternal, for it was not conceived in time and space.

Does any of this involve working with the poor, the sick, the orphans?

Many on earth are spiritually orphaned, poor, and sick. If you find it necessary to be a vessel for God through touch, prayer, silence, hands-on healing and loving in this manner, then be glad that your "way" has been made known to you. As you make use of the tools given you for healing, the small mind will lose its way and will no longer direct your path.

The other day when caring for the roses, I spontaneously began kissing them, seeing their radiant beauty within. The red velvet petals so luscious and soft kissed me back! I was amazed with these kissing flowers. I remembered what you said about giving "Life." It seemed as though these red roses literally were giving "Life" by giving of their Self.

*   *   *

Willingness

Yesterday, I was feeling in this ongoing darkness. I went to the gym and climbed up on the elliptical machine and began praying to the Holy Spirit that though I am receiving information, I am having difficulty applying it in my life. I asked the Holy Spirit to help for I was willing to recognize the Christ within every person in the gym. As I laid my eyes on each person, I easily sensed a peace within and around each one. I then saw Christ stationed all over the gym, standing by each piece of equipment. Christ was everywhere. I sensed the peaceful presence of Christ all over the building. What a gift.

Still today I sit in my choice to devote my life to God. What does this mean? Then I realize, God is within and my true nature is in union with God, hence my choice now becomes to devote my life to my true nature.

Make everything else a priority and the hidden nature of others will remain hidden. Their true nature will remain hidden. Herein lays judgment, grief, and secret despair.

Is it possible to be in the world, but not of the world?

Yes. Your nature, which belongs to God, finds expression in the world through you. Your work immerses you more deeply into God's presence as you become your work. It is not separate from who you are.

*   *   *

The Veil

Today a piece of clarity came. I was in the kitchen cooking dinner and watching television out of the corner of my senses. All of a sudden I heard that it was time. Instead of continuing to hang out in this place of feeling pulled to serve others as a vessel for God and at the same time struggling with the thought of how irresponsible this was, as in "you need to be working full time and saving money for your retirement," I realized it is time to follow the call. I have been trying to lead a "normal" life, but I do not believe in a normal life and I do not feel called to live a normal life. I feel called to serve the poor in spirit and those in real need, to serve however I am called.

I have reached my absolute end of being in this muddy pool year after year. I feel like an empty barrel with ropes tied around me. One rope is spinning me around in one direction and the other rope is spinning me around in the other direction, but neither rope is getting anywhere. I am just in a tizzy. This is useless toil. The Voice clearly told me that I can release myself from this turmoil by giving in to the longing to serve as a vessel for holiness. Then I thought that maybe after one year of devotion, I will just get it out of my system and go on with my life. Then I heard a still, small Voice say, "That will not happen, this is your life." Now I ask, "Who do I serve, how do I serve, and where do I serve?"

We are all called to serve; however, the greatest need can only be filled by God, Who remains present with us always. Service is the true hallmark of Divine Nature. The ultimate "reality" of this world hovers remarkably close to the veil surrounding the truth.

What does this mean?

We are incessantly seeking real love, but manage to find mostly that which only serves as an obstacle to real love. The greatest imposters reward us in ways that attract us ever more so to the veil, rather than the truth which lies behind it. Service is an opportunity to expose one's Divine Nature and see the veil for what it truly is, fear. In serving others your Divine Nature is exposed.

Once we recognize the real need in an individual we encounter the nature of the veil.

I thought the veil was fear. What is one's real need?

One's real need is to be reunited with Christ. The veil is one's choice to replace this real need with imposter needs of the world. This is a fear-based choice.

Maybe by serving the poor in spirit, my poor spirit will be served.

*   *   *

Elevating the Small Self

Why do I feel like I am having a more difficult time hearing you lately? What's up?

You remind me of a woman I once knew. She had a fierce strength and determination to serve others as her life's purpose. When the time came for her to begin her life's dream of opening up a wellness clinic for the poor, she became ill in her mind. Her vision became clouded and her unceasing headaches remained a source of difficulty for her.

What happened?

Her purpose was mutilated. She forfeited a life of vision for a role of sickness.

Why did this happen?

The vision of Christ became so out of the ordinary to her, so unlike the distant image she held in her mind and had grown comfortable with, that she could not place her trust in Christ's hands.

What do you mean by "out of the ordinary"?

Like a bird taking flight and leaving its own ways, its own body, and its own thoughts of itself behind on the tree limb to be free of its own limitations, she also started crossing such borders. She felt a sense of leaving herself behind and entering divine territory.

This morning in yoga class I sensed being in my body fully engaged in the yoga postures while also observing being outside the realm of my body. I feel like this woman you are talking about. Like the bird on the limb I was aware of my body on the yoga mat, yet I was merging with Spirit within and taking flight into a realm beyond my perceptions. I could feel the space between the two; between my body and the Spirit. What happened to this woman having these experiences?

Taking flight into the awareness of Christ is normal for one's Self, which resides there permanently. Once she decided that the feeling as if she was between floors on an elevator was too uncomfortable, she elevated her small self to a greater level of trust than Christ and lost her way.

Where is she now?

The mirror in your dressing room.

No wonder I felt such a kinship with her as you spoke. Yes, I have seen her around lately, out of the corner of my eye, on my face, in meditation, and in the faces of others, reflecting her self back to me. Yes, I have been feeling anxiety especially heightened during these past three weeks as I felt all of this rise up inside of me. A piece here, a piece there, in meditation and daily life. Okay, so now the puzzle has borders, in the sense that this all does not feel so unknown to me any more. The mystery of the awareness of Christ feels a miniscule less out of the ordinary. Let me rest here a moment please before flinging me in to the next realm. I feel blown away right now.

Let me remember your Self for you.

*   *   *

How do I Speak of This?

I realized today that one major obstacle I have encountered within myself is my reluctance to speak directly of my work being of service to Spirit through going to the Christ within. I want the message to be clear. How do I speak of this?

You have been so close to false doctrine for most of your life, that opening the door for fugitives running away from the lies of the world brings on hesitancy and confusion in you. It is not easy

to shake off the fluff of this world embedded in flesh for flesh's sake and be in Spirit for Spirit's sake. You are wanting to enter one's Spirit, but this world calls upon you in their flesh. Look at the one group of students you had who wanted to pull you more deeply into the flesh, but you would not go. The strength of God will carry you forward on this ministry, not your ideas.

I keep trying to figure out or imagine what a vessel for God does with her time. Where is the occupational description on this one? Of course I have conjured up many ideas. At first glance, they appear as creative, inspired ideas, then I am filled with doubt, followed by confusion. My brainstorming becomes a vicious cycle that literally gets me looped and entangled in an intricate web of knots, which manifests in my stomach. As I check in with Spirit, I understand that I need to be willing to "let God" and life will unfold accordingly.

These past few days I have been feeling a sense of butterflies in my stomach, as if something exciting is about to happen. Reminiscent of how I felt in grade school looking forward to going on a class field trip. I am realizing that being a vessel for God simply means letting my mind be healed moment-to-moment. This is an immense relief!

Once you begin to allow your healed mind to be shared with others, you will see the truth housed in everyone's healed minds.

How does this help them?

It shows them who they truly are.

*   *   *

Money Messages

I do not see how I have a right to ask for money as I allow myself to be a vessel for God when I do healing sessions, because I am not really doing the healing.

You are forgiving someone's perception of his or her self.

How am I to charge for this?

Money has been an obstacle for you. Remove the messages the world has given you about money and all of the monetary supply needed to perform God's work will be supplied.

So I need to give up my judgments and perceptions of money, having it or not having it, how to save it, how to spend it ... all of these preconceived notions are obstacles in my path in allowing my mind to be healed through the Holy Spirit.

*   *   *

Form Over Content

Mentor Within, I told John the idea of a "spiritual wellness" or "well-spirit" program. This would give one time to be in Stillness in many forms: walking a labyrinth, receiving therapeutic bodywork, movement, prayer, and meditation. He thinks that I am conjuring up all of these forms which have nothing to do with my true calling. Am I making all of this up instead of letting Guidance come through?

You have been doing God's work by simply allowing the green pastures of creation to solicit your compassion. God begs of you to follow through and let the Way transcend the utmost highs of the world, for you have asked for a freedom that lies solely in the hands of God. As you will relinquish your "freedom" in the world, you will find yourself passionate about one thing, serving God.

John is claiming that I am concerned with form and how it looks versus only the content. Sometimes I have tried to make it look a certain way as a marketing tactic and I have gotten lost in my mind because I get caught up in the way it is suppose to look. The emphasis becomes the form over the content. Now I have a real understanding that I need to get out of the way and let God work through me. I am totally willing to do this. I do want to reach out to others and be clear with others that I come to them so that we may both rest in God and allow our minds to be healed. Whatever this looks like, I am willing to do it, though I am drawn to nonverbal situations, as in bodywork and movement as avenues to "let go and let God." Am I wrong to want to bring this to others?

The body is not in and of itself a way to God. I want to be really clear with you; "hear." The body does not reside in the Spirit on any level. This is an important matter to address because others are somewhat confused here.

Does bodywork actually immerse one more fully in the physical and one's reliance on it?

You run the risk of strengthening one's belief in the body as a way to the Spirit. A person may spend their lives receiving bodywork and never open one's mind to God. You make the work spiritual by awakening to the Spirit within you and the person you serve.

I am not trying to discourage you, but just helping you to see that presenting yourself to the world as a bodyworker will then automatically cause you to be seen by the world as a bodyworker. You will therefore attract bodies that want you to work on them. People call plumbers when they need their pipes fixed. That is all I am saying. Either you are a bodyworker or a spiritual worker. Present your Self to the world.

What does a spiritual worker do?

A spiritual worker needs God to do the work.

What is "the work"?

Helping others to realize that they are lost and all of their efforts are being thwarted by their own insane belief that if they continue to search the world, eventually the questions will be answered and peace will be attained.

The secret of the spiritual journey is that it is not a search, or a quest; it is a state of mind. We do not have to find God. God simply is. God did not go anywhere. Do not waste more time on your spiritual journey looking for whatever it is you think you are supposed to find. Spend more time in the presence of God. Tell this to others.

Wow. I drop my pen and go into silence for awhile.

So, after all of my going this way and that as I trembled along my way on this spiritual journey, all of this time on a quest to find God somewhere, in something, in somebody; now here I sit. It is over. At approximately 8:03 p.m., Sunday, December 28, 2003, my spiritual journey as I knew it ended. I am in the presence of God, right here in my own backyard.

So I realized that all of these years that I have been searching for a form of life that would fulfill me, a life outside of me that would make my life complete, I was in fact searching for God. No wonder that no form ever quenched my thirst, ever satisfied my hunger, and always left me with lingering doubts. None of these things, activities, or people were what I was really searching for; nothing could take the place of the Kingdom of Heaven that lies within. I knew it existed. I never lost faith. I just never believed that it really existed within.

How does a person be in the world
but not of the world?

Chapter
Nine: January

**You are expressing
forgiveness in the world
by being a witness to the
presence of God within.**

Who Am I?

Today is a new day, a new year. This last year has been a doozy, so I cannot imagine the coming year. I suspect major life changes. Mentor Within, do you have any suggestions for me for the coming year? What can I expect?

Expect a miracle! Never see "happenings" just for what they appear to be on the surface. All interactions are superficial at best and require extreme sensitivity on your part to conquer the world of illusions and manifest security. Attract other listeners into your surrounding territory. Grace your presence on others who welcome Home for the sake of salvation of lost minds and sickened beings. We cannot lose that which we have already gained, for that which God gives no man may take away. All is well here.

Initiations seek new beginnings. Illusion's face cracks into several pieces so the hidden may be revealed. We place Light amidst the darkness. I Am is forever, but you are short-lived. Obnoxious sufferers for their own sake will perform rituals of rules and share their "talkings" as if someone is really listening, but I call upon you to abandon your self-sufficiency and start whole into life.

Denial is the source of nights, as daylight lengthens the day. Let yourself into the day with ease.

Mentor Within, thank you for listening to me. I wonder about the coming year and if I am to return to work at the hospital doing occupational therapy.

You are to return to the work of saving souls and reaching beyond the small mind's capacity. Scribes write letters to the One who knows better.

Write letters.

Am I a scribe?

Am I "I"?

Who do I write letters to and what for?

(No answer.)

What do you mean by "write letters"?

Letters will be written as you have already been given the words. The Scribe has sent you as a reader of the words given you. Remain in the envelope until you have read yourself.

Read myself?

Know thyself. You are the form; I Am the content.

What shall I do now? I feel a pull, but towards what?

Closer to God. Write the remainder of your life. It "becomes" you.

I saw God today in meditation. There I was, a log floating gently in the water and there God was, floating me.

Why am I?

Why am I?

I asked the question.

We have all asked the question.

So what is the answer? Why do I exist?

Already you know the answer. Tell me why you exist?

To fulfill my purpose of realizing and becoming who I Am.

*   *   *

Why the Holocaust?

Mentor Within, why the Holocaust, why the Jews, and why the ongoing anti-Semitism?

Bring this question into the Light.

What do you mean?

Bring this question to God.

Dear God, why did the Holocaust happen to the Jewish people? *(I now begin a conversation with God, in which I imagine, that the Mentor Within is assisting me in understanding God's responses.)*

Bringers of Light are often persecuted. Jesus brought Light into a world of confusion, pain, and darkness and he was never forgiven as the "Bringer of Light."

But many of the persecutors of the Jews claimed to be "Christians." Why would they persecute in the name of Jesus?

Many of the persecutors claimed to be human too.

What do you mean, of course they were human.

Though the body is an illusion, human nature, humanity, carries with it a divine nature. People who commit these kinds of acts have forgotten their divine nature. Jesus is someone they may look to in times of suffering and fear of death at their doorstep, but they actually fear Jesus; they fear his divine nature, their own divine nature.

So, you are saying that Jesus symbolized the divine nature in all of us, we fear this divine nature, and so we persecute it. Furthermore, Jesus was a Jew, so we hate the Jews for showing us, through Jesus, that God really does exist in our divinity?

Your truth is a breath of new air. Your understanding precise.

What about the persecution of the Jews before Jesus?

Rebels of the Light have known of the coming of Jesus long before his humanity manifested on this earth.

So, did you "send" Jesus to earth?

Jesus agreed to realize his divine nature thousands of years before he actually appeared in human form.

So, the choice was his?

Yes, choice is always yours.

So, why didn't he come much earlier?

Choice.

How in your sight did Jesus "realize his divine nature" on earth?

He let the peace of Christ rise out of him, after his birth, during his life, and after his death.

Who is "Christ"?

My "nature" available to all.

So, the Rebels of the Light, humans who have forgotten their divine nature, knew of the coming of Jesus and began killing Jews beforehand as a way to increase their power and maybe even to kill Jesus because they were not sure how this "Bringer of Light" would show himself on earth; as a kind of self-protection.

The Rebels of the Light know the darkness well and fear rules their minds. Chaos is their way — arbitrary, blind chaos planned out in illusion's details. Their microscopic world fears death, for it knows no Life, no union in God.

You have surely cleared this madness up for me. Thank you. So, what about the Jews at the time of Jesus who did not recognize him as the "Bringer of Light"?

Light acknowledges Light. Fear acknowledges darkness.

So, many were afraid.

Yes. Belonging to God may be a precious reality, but few choose the clarity.

What is the fate of the Jews?

Fate, as you speak of it, is man's choice.

So, you intervene by giving us a divine nature and we either choose our divinity, as Jesus did, or we cast it aside for the ways of fear. So, "i," my small self, cannot choose my divine nature?

Only Holy Spirit may choose our divinity for us. We are of weak minds and cannot reckon with our own divinity; thus, the Spirit of God serves us well as we selflessly take a moment of silence and immerse our fiery thoughts into the hands of Spirit. Let us remember the waters that heal, and in our remembering, the "i" can no longer sustain itself.

Beyond fear and doubt is your reason for living on this earth – to recognize your own divinity.

How do I move beyond fear and doubt?

Believe you can. There I Am.

What did you mean earlier, when you said that Jesus was never "forgiven" as the Bringer of Light?

He saw the Bringer of Light in others, his own Self in others, and they saw a man belonging to God and refused him. They refused God.

So, he was not received for who he really was, thus "unforgiven"?

Forgiveness realizes God within the Self.

So, persecution of the Jews continues because people have still not really seen the divine nature within themselves and though, apparently, they have seen the divine nature of Jesus who has forgiven them by seeing their divinity, they simultaneously hate Jesus, and therefore the Jews (generalizing to the entire Jewish population), for bringing forgiveness into the world through Jesus. Hatred of their own divinity has been projected onto Jesus and the Jews.

*   *   *

Claiming Our Divine Nature

Many disciples of Christ are needed to reveal divine territory to others.

What is "divine territory"?

People place themselves in divine territory when they reveal the "hidden" nature of God to those in darkness, through forgiveness.

So, it is like we are angry at Jesus for showing us our divine nature as Sons of God, because this challenges us to forfeit our ego minds and surrender into our divinity, the Kingdom of Heaven within. It is easier to say we "love" Jesus and worship him as an idol, as having attained something we could never attain. This is easier than claiming our own divine nature. This is the love-hate relationship at its epitome — no different than many of the relationships we have with each other here on this earth.

There is a big difference between Jesus lending us a hand by showing us the way, versus total dependence upon Jesus to save us from having to choose God over self, God over fear, God over hate. Jesus does recognize our divine nature, but we must choose to receive our divine nature. We fear receiving it because of what it might mean to our little lives, so we say "Jesus did it, he saved me from my self," so I do not have to give up my world and choose God.

Any other questions I should ask?

We will talk again. No matter, I Am with you. Remember Me.

I have made an observation. We look to other people, jobs, careers, material possessions, belief systems, values, our health ... to "save" us, and we "love" them when it seems to be working and we hate them when it seems to not be working. When they are "working," we tend to ignore, really hate, God because we are simply cherishing our self; when they are "not working," we turn to God in "love," really fear, because we realize we cannot keep our boat afloat alone. We will really only know love when we recognize our own divine nature in union with God.

Dear God, there is a lot of talk about Jesus in the above explanation realizing his divine nature. Not everyone believes that humans have a divine nature and they will defend their stance.

False humility comprehends at the levels of offensive and defensive. Such is the way of unbelievers. Christ shows the way out of this mess. You cannot accept your own belief system and Christ simultaneously. You will become hated by people who do not even know who you are.

I was hoping to be able to present this information in such a way that people could take it in as an explanation for and acceptance of their own divinity.

Accepting one's own divinity requires one's acceptance of Self.

Say more about "false humility."

Jesus humbled his false self to God, hence exposing his divine nature. False humility humbles itself to no one. Many are falsely humble.

Who are "unbelievers"?

Unbelievers are everyone who warrants proof of the existence of God in the material world.

How can I speak of Jesus having recognized his own divinity to those who believe otherwise?

Anyone may speak of one's belief system to me and I will find a way to shatter it in as much as you want it to be shattered. Truth is your reward.

So anyone devoted to truth and willing to surrender their own facts and figures, will be shown their divine nature in a way they can grasp it?

Powerful things happen when we realize truth matters more than history or ideas about history.

Mentor Within, are you still with me?

(Mentor returns.) Will you become a disciple of Christ?

Yes. What does that mean? Where is God?

God is listening. Disciples of Christ carry the Light into the world of unbelievers.

What about all of the people turned off by the words "Christ" and "Jesus"?

They will find another way. God will not forsake them. No one who wills their mind to God will be forsaken in the end.

So I need not worry about these terms offending people.

**You have enough to be. Prepare ye the way of the Lord.
The Risen Christ awaits all of those yet to come.**

*(God speaks.) Never worry or fear, my hand is upon you and
everything which you have no control over. Darkness shatters glass
dreams. My love for people frees people. Love Me, seek Me, and
teach others to do the same.*

Thank you again. My gratitude is immense.

*   *   *

The Denial of Self

I realized last night as I was falling asleep that I keep resisting my
Self and trying to replace my Self with what seems more appropriate
and aligned with socially acceptable ways, as well as my own rules
about how I "should" and "should not" be living. Then it hit me all
of a sudden how absurd this was. What if those individuals who have
chosen God over the ways of the world would not have done so — look
at what a loss of blessings this would have been.

Why do I keep insisting that I must live according to the ways of
the world, the ways of my profession, the ways of American women
striving to be superwoman? I was struck with a different answer this
time. Rather than thinking that I am messing up my life by not participating in the norm, I realize that I am denying who I Am if I participate
in the norm; I am denying my Self. This awareness of denial of Self
seemed much more insane and lethal than denial of my ego self in the
world. How crazy I thought. What if Jesus, the prophets, the seers of
God, the workers for God, and the mystics all chose to deny the Self?
What good or what purpose would they have served?

I will struggle until I just accept who I am. I am not referring here
to accepting my ego-centered idiosyncrasies, my personality. I feel a
strong sense of who I am and the calling I have heard and how absurd
it is to resist. No one will be served by my resistance.

*   *   *

Innocence

Mentor Within, this whole situation has arisen with two friends who are not wanting to bring a mutual friend into a gathering we have, a time for sharing and just getting a chance to see one another. I completely understand each of their reasons for wanting the group to remain just the three of us. Reasons like another person may take up too much time and space (energetically), concerns about confidentiality, just wanting the three of us to be together because we never see each other and they each see this other person at other gatherings ... you get the picture. Then I struggle with excluding a person who claims to be looking for spiritual sisterhood. I do not necessarily consider this a spiritual group, but more of a time for personal sharing and support. How do I handle all of this? The woman being excluded has spoken with me and though she has spoken with the others and understands their reasoning, she expresses hurt.

Look at the explanations that are being given and perpetuated because of three individuals' unwillingness to forgive a brother. You are convicting this person of being human.

I remember from the beginning feeling uncomfortable that this person was being left out, but even more uncomfortable that I had to keep the gathering a secret from her because we all knew that she would be upset about being left out. I agreed to all of this because I gave in to my ego telling me that I spend too much time alone and really should take advantage of this female gathering to be with friends. Apparently, on some level of consciousness I did not feel right about keeping this a secret and I blurted out about when the group will meet next, not fully aware that the excluded person was standing within hearing space. There went the secret and up came everyone's issues. I am not trying to be Miss Goody Two Shoes, I am confounded about how to deal with this situation. What if I lose these friends?

There go more minds separating from God. You can see the peace of Christ in everyone and all minds will be healed. I cannot protect you from your free will. You have a tendency to be a witness to other's small minds.

I wonder sometimes if I am moving beyond the level of ego-based friendships. Yet the whole world is ego-based, including me. How does a person "be in the world, but not of the world"? This seems impossible! In my experience some past friendships were fertile ground for judgments, gossip, complaining, and perpetuating the entanglement of the ego. This is a losing battle. I hate this, help.

You are attempting to battle the ego and you will never win this battle. Stop seeing the ego as innocent. You are very drawn in to wanting to see an individual's innocence, but it is the innocence of the ego which does not even exist, that you choose to see. This is how the ego pulls you in. See the innocence in who they truly are. Your true vision will be evident when you give your mind to God even though you are in the world.

How do I give my mind to God?

Practice. Practice. Practice. Like learning to ride a bike, when you fall off, get back on.

Do you recommend a specific form of practicing?

A teacher practices teaching. Teach others about God.

How do I teach others about God?

Be a witness for Self, not the ego.

I have been wondering about starting a group to read the text of *A Course in Miracles*, which I have not really read. Is this something I should do?

The text cannot be read solely for its own sake; it must be given to God for your understanding. True understanding will come only to those who want it. Clear your mind. Read the text. Give it to God. Read the Course alone. If others want to join you also, let it be.

Why do you stress that I read the Course alone?

Becoming a teacher of God requires tremendous study. You will gain a deeper understanding.

*   *   *

No Turning Back

I awoke this morning with fear in my belly. I immediately surrendered to God the day ahead of me, a typical day. Last evening as I was typing pages written months ago, I realized that I have been given answers to questions that I have been asking for 25 years. I just did not listen for the answers. While typing I felt enthralled, threw my hands up in the air and proclaimed, "I love you, God." My eyes opened this morning and "I love you, God" now felt like "Oh, God," as the fear of having been given the truth rose up inside of me. Now what do I do? Now I know that this vicious world is not God's place; it is not the real world. I know that I have been called to face reality and share the good news. I know that I cannot turn my back.

It is no accident that the next lesson in *A Course in Miracles*, "Illusions have been shattered," is literally a direct reflection of my experience. Amazing. Reality has landed right in my lap.

*   *   *

Ask This Question

How do I begin?

We begin to help those relishing the world. When masked faces go within and face the revealed corridors of their minds, they will change their path from false love to truth.

What are the "revealed corridors of their minds"?

The place where vision meets truth.

What is my role?

Your sole responsibility is to let yourself be saved. The mind that heals is healed. The mind that changes, changes minds. All in a day's work.

You will save yourself a lot of trouble if you stop letting your

little sick mind be pulled further into the world of terminal illness. There is no way out of fear except through Love.

Look past worldly ideas of ego love, love disguised. We can all list a series of behaviors and communication used as guidelines for being a loving person. Take that list and crumple it up and throw it away as far as your little mind can throw. This probably will not be far enough, as the ego has a far reach. We fight with our attempt to let go of that which we insist on being the way of human "respect." The more you attempt to throw the list away, the more it will come back to haunt you.

So how do I abandon this list of my concepts of love?

You do not. It abandons you just as the ego abandons you. It gives up in place of real love.

So, I do not attempt to abandon the ego?

No, this will maintain the struggle; ego battles ego.

Mentor Within, I am considering calling JoAnn, the director of pastoral care at the hospital, about ways I could provide spiritual service work. What do you suggest?

All kinds of work are necessary to fulfill the work of salvation. You cannot help but to be pulled in many directions now as you find a way of providing healing. Direct Service.

What is "Direct Service?"

We often return to our Source for replenishment and nourishment. Helping others with their salvation requires that you be filled with the Holy Spirit. Your fear gets generated as you try to make decisions alone.

I understand all of this. What is "Direct Service"?

How can I help? Ask this question a thousand times a day. You will be given a direct answer.

*   *   *

Homeless mind

I have sunken into the deep, dark secrets of the ego mind. I am lost. Mentor Within, how can I ever heal others and bring Light to others if I am in darkness? I hear all of your wonderful words and know their truth, but I fall again and again and again into the darkness. What am I doing wrong?

One can enter this place of darkness from which you speak when life is unable to keep up with us.

What do you mean?

Meandering around the Self are the highly charged activities of human consciousness. Self recognizes divinity and envisions more appropriate interactions for you. You have become entangled in inappropriate activities.

What "inappropriate activities"?

Locked inside the doors of the fearful mind is the self that harbors guilt and death forever. Nothing in the world will save you from this unreal twist of fate. Nothing could be further from the truth that your little mind, which is homeless, can provide you with shelter and the love you crave. Enduring the little mind, yours and others, is not a meaningful life; for all purposes it is death. Only God can issue freedom. When your consumption of the world fulfills its empty promises and your hands are raw from searching through the brittle bones, brokenness, and scorched dreams, and the darkness has become more of itself, we will wade through the swamp together and I will lead you to Presence. Here will you be fulfilled.

It seems like the more I am around people, the more I get pulled into the littleness and lost sense of the world. Then I say to myself, "What was that? What did I just say? What did I just agree with?" It is a trap! I feel like I am in a house of mirrors and hallways with tilted ceilings and warped floors. I enter the front door, and by the time I reach the exit I do not know which end is up. It all happened so quickly, as if behind my back and without my permission. Where did

I go? Who was that I just pretended to be? I did not mean any harm, I was just socializing and trying to be nice. You know the story. A part of me wants to just say, "You know I do not participate in these kind of activities and conversations any more." I cannot imagine any human being who has truly given their mind to Holy Spirit participating in so many of these hideous conversations like I have with people. So, it is one thing to have been given the truth, it is quite another to live it, moment-to-moment.

*   *   *

Death

Sometimes I see myself working with the sick and the poor because I imagine they are less caught up in the material endeavors of the world; life is one day at a time. Or maybe working with the dying to usher them out of this world.

Death is also a trap of the illusion, as if it brings freedom. It does bring freedom from the life we once knew, but it is not enough to die. The hallmark of life in Christ is not to be released into death; it is to be released into Life. In working with the dying you do not want to emphasize that dropping the body is the way out. It is not the way out. Going within is "the way."

*   *   *

The Darkest Dark

The more I go within I still fall into the ways of the world and it seems that I am falling deep into a darker darkness than before when I was less aware of the truth.

This is only the beginning of coming to know the truth, that dark appears to be at its darkest. You fall more deeply because you have risen more highly, if you will. It is a lesson to teach you the stark contrast between Light and darkness. Nothing remains

the same once you have gone before God and basked in God's Light; nothing remains as it was once before, nothing remains the same. Only truth will save you now and you know it. This is not an easy place to remain for long, but it is important to your learning the distinction between life and Life in Christ. I will not bear the darkness for you. I will be the same Light every time you choose to return until you return and leave no more.

You mean I have to bear the darkness all alone?

Together are we always. The darkness feels alone, that is its ugly purpose, and hence you bear it alone. I am inside of you the whole length of the darkness, but you are facing outwards. Go inside.

*   *   *

The Call of the Self

Wow, what a miracle, every day a miracle. As I meditated, I saw my family pure, new, and full of Light, as if a halo were around each of their heads. Then Albert floated into my thoughts. I saw him sitting in front of me and I called on God for his healing and I did healing work around him. It was amazing. I fell into such a state of focus. Ah, finally focused. All that mattered for twenty minutes was Albert's healing. I heard myself praying over him, "I am healed and whole." I felt completely blessed by Albert. I saw him as healed and whole and I felt healed and whole. While in this place, my phone rang and it was Albert leaving a message.

Three hours later I was at Zoya's for lunch. The owner, a vivacious Russian woman, and I somehow got into a conversation about God and spirituality. I feel we each blessed the other and encouraged one another to turn to God within and listen.

These are the days to write about and share your experience of facing and meeting the Christ within.

I realize that insofar as reaching out to others, the choice is mine.

God will not force me to do the work. I must choose the Light. I choose the Light. Why does a part of me want to begin this ministry and another part hesitates?

Being aware of the calling and becoming the call are not two separate events, and you are trying to treat them as such. The call has gotten your awareness. You became the call when you answered with your awareness. However, you are still trying to turn your back on the call, which is not possible without mental strain, because you cannot turn your back on your Self. Your Self is who you are. Everything is backwards. Your attempt to "become" your Self is thwarting your efforts to reach out to others because you have not yet recognized that you already are your Self. There is nothing to become.

You are waiting for something to happen — for you to wake up one day and feel free, then ready to save others from their prison. You are already free. Now act upon your freedom, in the world, or in solitude. The choice is yours. You accept or not accept, that is it.

I want to share this freedom and sense of Self that I experience while in solitude. I want to take it to others so that they may have their own experience. What would this look like?

Do not worry about what it will look like. Once you step one foot into and enter the building, your mission will already be accomplished, because You have arrived in recognizing that You have arrived. What we spoke of earlier: you have nothing to become. You already are that which you are striving to become.

Okay. I finally get your point. This process of me stepping out into the world is for me to recognize who I already am. Apparently, I still think I need to work on who I Am. Now that is funny.

You are devoted to bringing the healing presence of God to others, so others may find this presence within themselves. You are expressing union with God. You will know what is needed when you walk in the door. You provide what is needed in the moment, nothing more. You have been called to serve the poor, sick, and the poor in spirit. This is your calling and you have

**answered your call. If they do not want you there, then go on
to the next place. Your call will be answered.**

*   *   *

Forgiveness

**You are expressing forgiveness in the world by being a witness
to the presence of God within.**

*   *   *

Longing

Mentor Within, in meditation and prayer this morning I had a
sense that maybe this whole "calling" thing is just my idea. What makes
me think I am so special as to be called to do anything. I mainly feel
God calling me towards a deeper union, but this is really the only "true
calling" I have sensed. I have felt a longing to help the poor, sick, and
the poor in spirit, but is a longing within the same as a calling? I do not
want to supercede God's Will for me.

**Once you have started to feel your Self in deep union with
God, you automatically long for others to experience this same
deep union. Your longing to serve the poor, sick, and those poor
in spirit is a longing for deep union with God, the same as your
call. There is no difference.**

I hear you telling me to be in deep union with God and to invite
others into that space — rest here. Who are the sick I am to work with?

**The sick and the dying are all of those who have lost contact
with God, who have forgotten the love that God's Presence
provides. We are all dying once we have forgotten.**

Albert came into my mind during meditation this morning. I felt
an incredibly powerful Light around him and the presence of God

very strong around him; his physical body disappeared, revealing only Spirit. I felt totally blessed by God in Albert's presence.

After a precious time of meditation and prayer, during which I felt the healing power within and saw healing and wholeness in others, I went full swing into impatience and judgment, from one extreme to the other. When I let my small mind go to work, all I see around me are small minds. When I let my Self be seen, all I see around me is the Self in others - simple, but not easy to put into practice. It makes my life a lot easier when I am sweet and kind. Yet there is a fine line between the sweet kindness of the small mind and the sweet kindness of the Self. There is an effort and fakeness that goes into the sweet kindness of the small mind, as well as a sense of attachment to controlling another's behavior.

*　　*　　*

Anger

I ask myself what did I learn today from the rough spots I pounced over. I learned that my ego thoughts are like a black hole that suck me in, bound and determined to prove to me that I am not connected to God and even that there is no God. I know this is not true.

Better to have a bad day and eventually recognize the presence of God than to have a good day all on your own.

You are brilliant!

Reflecting God within will provide in every instance.

Releases of anger that you are experiencing are the small self's way of holding on for fear of annihilation. The ego experiences itself as shrinking. It draws attention and focus onto itself to prevent you from your healing role in the forgiveness of the world.

What can I do about this?

"I walk into the Light" is a good mantra to use with thoughts that pull you into the darkness.

I dread this emptiness inside.

Penetrate the emptiness and you will stumble upon a treasure of gold. You will find what you have been looking for; you will find God. You will then come to serve God. You have been avoiding what you think is emptiness. Go deeper now. Fear will arise; go deeper still. Let yourself go deeper into the fullness of Silence within.

*   *   *

Missing God

I rested my body and soul down this morning for meditation and prayer. No sooner did I sit down, than I felt an "absence" and without thought uttered the words "I miss You." Tears turned into audible crying into longing as I realized that I missed God. Never have I had such an experience of missing God. Yet once I spoke the words "I miss You," the absence was filled with Presence. Yesterday I was unable to spend time writing and I was aware of this absence during the day. How did I come to this place of missing God, such an unusual place?

Once you have received God's graces, you have entered into an understanding upon which all of your substance rests. Let not yourself be deceived by mirrors. Look (instead) directly into the face of God and perpetuate the truth as it has been explained to you. You will begin to notice now when you have surrendered to the world, for it is a stark contrast to surrendering to God. You are now less susceptible to defending your ego ideas and more willing to rest in the hands of God.

Much earlier you spoke of the "Church of the Healing Waters." Is this really a church?

It is a traveling healing center serving others in need of Christ's healing. Let me explain this further now that you are ready. The packaging, if you will, of Christ's healing is you; you and those you serve form the church. The church begins when

you begin; it is not an entity outside of you and your work. It is you and those you serve.

How do I make a living at this?

Perform the necessary tasks which offer you freedom and release — meditation and prayer, serve those willing to receive, regain awareness by losing your self, and have mercy and forsake judgment, for yours is a life for Christ. "Living" has a different meaning in your world than it does in mine.

What about serving those unwilling to receive?

Take hold of their minds and cast out the weariness that prevents them from reaching out for God.

How do I do all of this?

Pray around them and see their weariness as an obstacle rather than impenetrable resistance. Nothing gets by God. Eventually, all will have to come to God.

What about selling a healing program and negotiating my pay?

The price of Christ is high, the cost of healing beyond the treasures of this world. No one among the wealthy is rich enough to buy it. Let those who choose to pay do so, as this is their method, and we each have our own path to God.

What is the cost of healing that even the wealthiest cannot buy it?

Willingness to let God in. The gates of Heaven are within. Will you let God in?

*　　*　　*

Hotel Bliss

I recall a dream last night in which I was in a small, dingy bar with a few other people. The owner kept answering the phone, "Hotel Bliss, the world's largest, most beautiful ... hotel," as if it was the Ritz Carlton.

"Is he crazy," I thought, "this place is a dive and it is not even a hotel."
What does this dream mean?

**This man is seeing what is within, beauty and grandness, and
has opened himself up to serving others and welcoming others
into this "bliss." He truly believes that he is the owner of a big,
beautiful hotel. He sees what is within, certainly a man of faith.
You and your corroborating friend in the dream represent the ego
who believes that you, as the space for "Healing Waters," are less
than perfect. You are not seeing what is within; you are looking
outside.**

Now I see my predicament. I see myself like the bar, as less than a
perfect specimen to ever channel healing love or to ever invite others
into. I am waiting for this beautiful and grand thing outside of myself
to manifest before I even begin serving others. I see the need to have
vision like the bar owner in this dream.

My mind is moving swiftly through
the Rolodex of worldly solutions and
I am clear that there are none.

Chapter
Ten: February

The greatest achievement
the body can accomplish
is to let the Spirit have its
Way.

The Crucifixion

I began listening and writing this book because I was not happy being "content."

As I was falling asleep these words fell from my lips, "Dear God, I see no life for me without You."

Today I told my mother that I am taking this year to listen for God's plan for my life and that I may be doing some volunteering. She is the first person I have told this to. This is an odd time. I feel in limbo. Have you any words?

A spiritual place.

As you say this, I am seeing an area of stone as if within a cave. Within the stone is a circular deepening from which steam arises, like something is brewing. What is this?

This is a better place for you.

What do you mean?

One finds answers to life's questions here.

Where is this place?

Enter.

Enter? Where? What? How?

The realm of no physical senses, no touch, sight, taste, smell, or hearing.

How do I as a body full of sensations enter such a place? I have no frame of reference for such a place.

There is no pain here. Pain has been your enemy, disguised as friend. Be not a friend to such for it has ears that do not hear and eyes that do not see. Pain traverses dark alley ways and you get lost on your way to God.

Pain is real, or so it seems. It is like an anesthetic numbing joy. Pain forms bonds as pain attracts pain. Sometimes I feel I have been addicted to pain, that I am pain. Pain has been there for me, acknowledging my existence. What do I do with all of this?

Remove the suffering.

How do I do this?

Remove the suffering mind. Mind suffers over pain which it experiences, seeks, and fixates upon and then seeks pleasure to relieve itself of the pain. This often exacerbates the pain and suffering in the end.

Why would I seek pain and suffering?

You have learned and taught it to be the way to truth. Suffering is the human condition from which it is believed the only salvation is death, either physical death and/or the death of the crucifixion.

Jesus' crucifixion?

It began with him. Jesus did not belong to death through the crucifixion, rather he belonged to the resurrection in Christ and he knew it.

Must he have gone through the crucifixion to belong to the resurrection?

The cross Jesus carried burdened him until his death. At his crucifixion he surrendered his cross to God.

What was his cross to bear?

Bearing the truth.

How is bearing the truth a cross?

It is a responsibility.

So Jesus' cross was bearing the truth and once he bore that truth, he gave it back to God in exchange for his freedom not of this world?

Jesus was free in the world to the extent one can be; his mind was free.

So (my) physical death or Jesus' crucifixion will not set my mind free of pain and suffering?

Ask God to identify you with the Christ mind.

I keep seeking solutions to this painful mind in this world. My mind is moving swiftly through the Rolodex of worldly solutions and I am clear that there are none. How do I ask God to identify me with the Christ mind?

"I want to know God" has been your prayer. Now pray, "I want to know who I Am."

*   *   *

Between Two Worlds

Today I realize that I am happy to be alive. At the same time I feel myself walking the ledge between two worlds. People ask me questions and speak to me of this world. I listen and respond the best that I can, considering the fact that I know people are searching for happiness that can only be found within. It may appear that they want a shiatsu treatment or be prescribed certain foods to eat, but I sense the urgency underneath the surface. On some level of consciousness they have yet to find peace, and time appears to be running out. I sense the preoccupation with the physical world. At the same time I see more than what the naked eye reveals. I see the love of God radiating through them which they have yet to find because of their external search.

So, yes, I walk the ledge between two worlds. I play in both worlds. I watch both worlds. I ponder both worlds. Where do they meet?

Between Heaven and earth lies a human being who has yet to learn that while his body is anchored to the density of the material world, the Spirit rests peacefully and moves with great ease all around him.

Where do body and Spirit meet?

I am seeing a body walking around the darkness of a cave looking for something, but it does not know exactly for what it searches. The body grows colder and hunched over, now walking on its tiptoes attempting to avoid the thorns beneath its feet. Eventually the calloused body dies, still searching for something it could never find. I do not see the Spirit anywhere with the body in this darkness.

Where is Spirit?

Spirit lies ahead, but the body never makes it as it blindly travels and searches in the darkness for the Light.

Once again, where do body and Spirit meet?

The greatest achievement the body can accomplish is to let the Spirit have its Way. I mindfully "make use" of the body when I deem it necessary to transfer a message to the individual in the body or on to another individual. The body will simply follow the rules of the ego mind or one can let Spirit use it as a manifestation of Self. I love you and will never abuse your body the way the ego mind will. There is a transfer of training that one must undergo from the ill will of the ego mind to the transcendent love of the Spirit-Mind.

What is the Spirit-Mind?

The Mind within, which recognizes its Self residing in Spirit.

CONCLUSION:

February 25, 2004

A Conversation with Jesus

I long to know. I ask Jesus himself, "Who is the true Jesus the Christ and what spiritual beliefs do you want me to follow?"

Jesus the Christ was the Son of Man who came to lay claim on the world of deceit, casualness about fidelity to God, and foul language, those words that are not of God, but of the human predicament and are spoken in the name of God as if the words of God. Jesus the Christ acknowledged the power of the Holy Spirit in his life and passionately embraced the Spirit of truth with his fellow beings, though many were unable to listen for themselves. He shined a Light in the darkness of souls, forgiving them by seeing their ability to perpetuate love over hate. Jesus the Christ I Am.

Not a creature of flowery fantasy. I too needed to be cast out of the valley of the shadow of death by Christ. I too have fallen prey to doubt, worry, and sin. I too felt the excruciating pain of self-hatred and contempt for others. I suffered on the cross before I ever made it to the cross.

I suffered daily over my own incompleteness as I chose to live without God as my true Father and Mother. I suffered immensely under the rule of my shadow that foresaw only evil and fallen nature for me. There was no hope for me in my enslavement in the world or in my mind. The snake pit awaited me, for I saw it with my own eyes. I awaited the presence of God as I realized that the only way out was down into the depths of my eternal soul. I fell before God and begged for my forgiveness and the forgiveness of those who had gone before me. I played out the fall of man in the world and rise of man in God.

My far distance that I traveled towards God took me on a long journey. I chose the long way Home; not everyone saw what I saw. There is no short cut to God, though we each have our own route. My message was one of freedom from the world. I had a license to forgive as I begged for God's mercy on my own soul.

I never founded any religions or denominations. It was not my role to rule the world, but rather to see the world for what it was and heal those willing to escape into God. It was not until my middle age that I saw what was going to happen to me. I struggled with the surrender into God's Will. I fought the battle daily, never failing to surrender in God's eyes.

Several years ago I remember walking into my apartment, bursting into tears and dropping to the ground at the foot of my bed. Flooded with the remembrance of Jesus' life, death on the cross, and resurrection, I suddenly was washed over with the realization that Jesus knew me. He knew me even before I was born. In that moment I felt Jesus standing beside me and offering forgiveness — he was seeing me for who I truly am. As I was seen in the light of innocence, I was filled with the Presence of God's Love. Love was palpable as It consumed the room and I was filled beyond measure. This was a profound experience as it came out of context and seemed to have a meaning beyond which I could comprehend in that moment. A meaning beyond the traditional meaning many have given Jesus' life and death. Jesus, what was the meaning of this experience?

**I knew you before you were born because I knew myself as
human and struggling in the world as you, as all of us humans do.
I died on the cross for the people who did not know that salvation
comes from Christ. I am just a man. Many others besides the Jews
needed salvation. I carried the message of Christ and this was my
cross: to bury the old messages and bring forth the message of
Christ into the world, though many would become disenchanted
with me. I am the one chosen for the work because I was willing
to do the work to prove that Christ heals, Christ saves. We are
not all chosen to carry the message of Christ into the world; not
all are able to render themselves willing for such a surmountable
task of bringing a cure to the illness of the world, which is the
loss of one's own sense of being connected to the Spirit of God.
Few are called to carry the message of Christ into the world
because few choose to listen. Christ calls everyone forth
to salvation, but not everyone is expected to minister Christ
to the world. I Am.**

You call curing the illness of the world a "surmountable" task?

**When addressing this issue your focus is to be on the root
cause of all illness, not the symptoms, which remain insurmountable
and quite disturbing to the population.**

Who else has been called to minister Christ to the world?

**Ministering Christ to the world is about sharing Christ as
Healer with others. Too many get caught up in evangelizing,
preaching and talking about salvation.**

What is wrong with evangelizing and preaching the Christ message
and talking of salvation?

Nothing, if you have been given permission by God to do so.

Why would we not all be given permission?

**Salvation awaits those who follow Christ, not those who
crucify Christ.**

What do you mean by "crucify Christ"?

To erect fortresses and buildings in my name and forge "knowledge" of my life and message is the crucifixion of Christ. To be instruments of fear rather than engendering love is the crucifixion of Christ. We use fear in countless ways to undermine God's Will. Hence, few are called to minister Christ to the world.

We must have a lot of false ministry going on then.

In the name of God.

Though few are called into ministry, I assume everyone is called to love like Christ in the world. Is this true?

Everyone is called to the reality of Christ in their lives and the lives of one another. The mystery of Christ is revealed here as we walk amidst the poor, the sick, and the poor in spirit, helping everyone to gather the riches of God within their reach. Come in to your Self and the Self in others and you have come in to Christ.

Am I called to minister Christ to the world or only to love like Christ?

You have been called to minister Christ into the world in a most unusual way.

What is this unusual way?

I am liberating you from being a teacher of worldly students into being a teacher of Godly students. Meaning that those who wish to procrastinate their call to God will not arrive at your doorstep. Only those wishing to manifest their Godly nature in the world will be calling on you. You have been called to minister and to love, for you know it is a surmountable task; your faith becomes you.

(I now turn to the Mentor). Mentor Within, what is "salvation?"

Salvation is recognizing who you think you are and then pulling off the bandages, as if opening your eyes for the first time, and coming to see who you really are — one Self in God.

Why do I need salvation?

You need salvation from your own self.

Why do I need salvation from my self?

Precisely because you do not know why you need salvation from your self.

What? This is a bit of circular reasoning, don't you think?

The self-reliance of the false self carries messages back and forth from one aspect of the false self to another aspect of the false self, within you and between yourself and others.

So, the false self operates within a closed system existing within its own perceptions. Hence, we need salvation from our perceptions.

Because they are your own perceptions.

What are wrong with my perceptions?

They are not real. You put them in service of the self. Christ calls you to offer your Self to others, this is your service.

(I return to my conversation with Jesus).

What spiritual beliefs do you want me to follow?

I will give you the real Bible message if you want it?

Yes, I do.

Begin by writing down what you now believe about Christ.

I believe Christ is my salvation from my false self.

I believe Christ acknowledges the existence of my Self.

I believe Christ will not interfere with my own free will.

I believe Christ loves me and everyone.

I believe Christ Heals others and myself.

I believe Christ listens to me.

I believe Christ is the pure Light shining forth
in the world.

I believe we all need salvation from our errors and mistakes to feel our wholeness.

I believe Christ wipes away my fear-based thoughts of who I am.

I believe Christ sees me for who I am, even when I am lost in the valley of the shadow of death.

So, what is the Bible message?

Everything that has to do with Love, has to do with Christ.

What about all of my beliefs about Christ?

Love is the message.

Do I share these beliefs with others? Are these the spiritual beliefs that you want me to follow?

I want you to follow Christ. Do not attempt to perpetuate more beliefs. Action will speak for you.

So, regarding the message of Jesus being our savior and worshipping him for salvation, what Jesus do you have to say of this?

I am the Way, the Truth, and the Life as I Am in Christ. I Am resurrected in Christ through everyone who chooses to follow Christ. Everyone who chooses "Christ" chooses salvation. I am a man; worship me and truth will befuddle you, for I am only the truth as I am resurrected in Christ. Every time anyone follows Christ there is a resurrection of one's soul. I am here as a Teacher of God to show the way — nothing more, nothing less.

How do I follow Christ?

Right now.

Okay, but how?

Minister to everyone's salvation. Respond regularly to calls for help. As you receive My love, I Am the Light of the world.

My core is alive for I am seeing my Self and receiving the message to be Christ in the world. Every call for help is a call for salvation. This is not a message of the world, but a message of healing for the world. I will give healing as I receive it and I will receive healing as I give it. Giving thanks.

Amen.

Epilogue:

Mary Gerard

Lesson Learned:
"Let Your Self Be Seen."

During the past nine months recorded above, I made a conscious choice to turn up the volume on thoughts that were running and often ruining my life. Then I became quiet and listened for the still, small Voice of inner wisdom. Clearly I heard them both, the voice of fear and the Voice of Love.

What is the point? The point is to observe the false self and to unravel this fearful self and its sabotaging thoughts. Why? Not to replace them with new and improved more positive and uplifting thoughts, for these are only the flipside of the sabotaging thoughts. I was not interested in flipping the coin which could easily be flipped again, but in tossing out the coin. My longing was giving my self over to Spirit for healing and awakening to the Spirit within, who I truly am. I am the thought of God. I am the perfect love of God. We all are. This is the Self.

Why go through this long, arduous process? How could I not. With each unraveling of who I thought I was, should be, or was trying to become, I caught a fleeting glimpse of who I really am. Our Self wants to be known, wants to be seen. This process of "undoing" is a necessary part of coming into the awareness of Self. The demons, recognized for what they are, our fearful thoughts, must then be surrendered to Spirit, for where the Light shines, there is no darkness.

These nine months and the time since then have been remarkably different. Sure my ego still tries to get its two cents in, I have not fully given my mind to God. The change that has taken place is that now I recognize mine and others fearful perceptions. Now I want to surrender these perceptions to Spirit for healing versus reacting out of habit, social expectations, defensiveness, self-protection, and worldly "love." All of these reactions are fear-based. We develop a familiarity with these reactions which provides a certain level of "comfort." I have found real comfort by letting go of how I think things should be and receiving a new vision of life. Even when I forget to give my thoughts over and hold on tightly to the reins of control, now I remember much sooner to let go. I notice the lack of peace and realize, "something is not right here."

At times, I am willing to receive Grace, no work required on my end. These times are becoming more and more frequent as I realize, Grace is always given. More of the time I am choosing to be vigilant of my thoughts as I am recognizing perceptions keeping me locked in fear. By the way, fear does not necessarily look like something out of a horror flick, catching me off guard and causing a dramatic reaction. Fear can be as benign as me feeling peeved that someone did not return my phone call or is late for dinner. Even behavior appearing loving like paying someone a compliment or doing a friend a favor can be fear-based. Fear is acting out of the false self, rather than the true Self. Now I am willing to wake up to who I truly am. This is forgiveness. This is freedom.

It is worth pointing out here that when I began this process, I was not looking to replace my current life with an 8 x 10 glossy of the new me and my "transformed" world. A better illusion, a makeover, would no longer satisfy. So, I cannot honestly now share with you seemingly impressive things like: a boosted financial portfolio, a new and improved soul mate, a perfected physique, a higher IQ, living in incessant bliss .... I am a human being. I get out of bed, face the day, put one foot in front of the other, put my foot in my mouth, fall down, get up, and just live life. The difference is that my desire is no longer to be misled through life by the false self; doing life my way. Instead, I walk hand in hand with Spirit, when I choose. Now I see that I have a choice, that I have another way to see. Now I let my Self be seen. This is peace. This is joy. This is love.

Seeing My Mother Truly

By the way, on my birthday this past July, I met my mother and father for lunch. As my mother walked towards me her head hanging down, she apologetically said, "Well, I don't have a gift for you." Spontaneously, as if without thought, the words flowed off my lips, "You are my gift." I felt a release of joy and love for my mother unlike that which I have ever felt. My mother lifted her gaze towards me and with a look of surprise on her face and the sound of joy in her voice, she exclaimed, "Ohhh, thanks!" We embraced.
It's a miracle! Spirit does move us if we are willing to be moved.

My lesson learned:

Let Your Self Be Seen.

Life will be easier, Love will be simpler.

Epilogue:
The **Mentor Within** Speaks

I am of Extraordinary means; God is my means, I am God's plan. We are all God's plan. Once we actually agree to God's plan, we know these things, for we know God; we know our Self, that part of us still joined with God. Our little ego selves fall away from sheer lack of attention. The ego would not recognize Love if it walked in front of it and caused the ego's grocery bag mind to spill all of its contents. After all, there is still the bag, eagerly waiting to be filled by still more of the "self-fulfillment" preached by the world. The whole mind must be relinquished to God, bag and contents.

As God sees it, there are only two ways out of the mind and in to Love: forgiveness and surrender. Obstacles to forgiveness and surrender, thus Love, include: self-hatred, judgment, cruelty, self-aggrandizement, innocence taking on the form of guilt, and the "truth" of the small self disguised as Love. This is the utmost blasphemy: selling our God-given souls to the beckoning ugliness of the world when all we really have to give is Love. All we are is Love. Be Love Now. Let your Self be seen and I will be seen along with you.

Immense joy and laughter comes from such Self-giving. Teach what you know, not what you have learned. Cure what ails you; temporary satisfaction is not a cure. Real healing comes from blatantly declaring salvation for your self by reaching outside of your small self for God and then finding your Self waiting patiently, with a smile on Its face, within you. Nothing outside of your Self will save you, for it is all a projection of blank pages we have filled in with our own noise. There is a place within where only Silence rests — the melody of God, the rhythm of Love, the cadence of forgiveness. The power of Silence within is beyond the teacher of a thousand words.

Recognize the mirror of this world that deceives you. Place it on the mantle with your other petty treasures to be dusted and admired from afar. Now sit. Go within. Fear not what you leave behind, for it is fear itself. Behind the eyes of the soul is the vision of God. Now see for your Self what really matters. Beyond the echoes of the "love" of the ego past, present, and future is the Gift of Life. When you are ready and willing, I am here for you. I await your presence. I am the Voice of your true Self who knows All. I Am.

Some chances, opportunities as you name them, come only once in a lifetime, once in a blue moon. I come every minute of your day, every blink of your eye.

Everywhere you stand, there I Am.

Let Your Self Be Seen

and

I Will Be Seen Along With You.

*FOOTNOTE, p. 93, Mentor Within, please speak to the statement, "Those who seek not to offend God."

Guilty witnesses to Divine imperfection, which does not really exist, find it difficult to imagine a God that cannot be offended, because they feel offended by others who are not in agreement with their image of God.

A Healing Practice

"to heal, bless, and comfort"

The willingness to be silent, listen, and awaken to the Holy Spirit within, brings healing, blessing, and comfort.

On a journey so profound and Life giving, I long to share the healing presence of the Divine available to all. Healing sessions begin with quietly centering our minds on God, inviting Holy Spirit in for healing, and expressing our willingness to be healed.

Through silent prayer, meditation, and a healing touch, we hear the Voice within reminding us who we truly are, the perfect love of God. I am a witness to the presence of God within. Here, healing happens.

Amidst the illusion of brokenness that can feel very real and keep us suffering, searching, and disillusioned, spiritual healing is offered. As one surrenders the false self to God, healing affirms the truth that we are already complete, experienced as the sweet rest in Divine hands.

Receiving a healing session is Grace filled for giver and receiver, opening the door to a personal experience of being safe, healed, and whole.

PROJECT
HEALING

Blessings offered by Spirit

Spiritual

> * Taking part in your healing
> * Awareness of Loving Presence
> * Movement along your spiritual path
> * Opening your mind to forgiveness of self and others
> * Joy
> * Peace

Though not the central focus of a healing session, one often experiences relief, release, and calming on physical, mental, and/or emotional levels. These benefits vary among individuals, yet may manifest as:

Physical

> * Promoting health and well being
> * Falling away of symptoms

Mental

> * Calming the mind
> * Awareness
> * Clarity
> * Happiness

Emotional

> * Balance
> * Lessening of anxiety
> * Lightness

To schedule a healing session with Mary Gerard you may refer to her website: thementorwithin.com

INDEX

To order additional copies of

The *Mentor* Within: Let Your SELF Be Seen

visit http://www.thementorwithin.com

To purchase by Mail Order
The Mentor Within
P.O. Box 9235
St. Louis, MO 63117

$19.95 includes shipping and handling

Please make checks or money orders payable to
"Project Healing"

PROJECT
HEALING
PRESS